THE SARTHE TRAMWAYS

AN INTRODUCTION TO THE TRAMWAYS DE LA SARTHE

PETER SMITH

COPYRIGHT 2016 Peter Smith

ISBN –13: 978-1523264360

ISBN-10: 1523264365

Loué. — Le Pont de la Tuilerie

St-RÉMY-DES-MONTS - Gare des Tramways

CONTENTS

INTRODUCTION   PAGE 4

THE SARTHE DEPARTMENT   PAGE 7

THE STANDARD GAUGE RAIL NETWORK.   PAGE 8

THE DEVELOPENT OF THE TRAMWAY SYSTEM   PAGE 11

LOCO'S AND ROLLING STOCK.   PAGE 18

CIVIL ENGINEERING   PAGE 23

THE TRAMWAY ROUTES:

1. LE MANS   PAGE 29
2. LOUE & ST JEAN SUR ERVE   PAGE 39
3. LA FLECHE & MAYET.   PAGE 52
4. CHATEAU DU LOIR, LA CHARTRE & ST CALAIS.   PAGE 66
5. MONTMIRAIL & MAMERS   PAGE 83
6. SEGRIE & ALENCON.   PAGE 103

INTRODUCTION.

In 2003 a book was published in France by Claude Wagner which described the Sarthe tramways in impressive detail. However to the best of my knowledge nothing has ever been written about then in English, and though Wagner's book is a superb piece of work it is not easy to follow unless you have very good French. I hope this book will give readers in the UK the opportunity to discover this fascinating metre gauge system, and having done so of course then buy Wagner's book as well!

The problem Claude Wagner had is that the Sarthe system was large and sprawling, probably the most comprehensive unified narrow gauge network in France, and he covered the history, loco's and stock , engineering and each line in turn in one large volume. This meant that the station picture tended to be very small which I find frustrating as they are what interest me the most! This book therefore takes a different approach as there is no point covering the same ground; following a brief description of the system I will look in as much detail as possible at each line in turn . The Sarthe network was not particularly well covered by the postcard publishers and unfortunately some stations seem to have passed without being recorded at all but there are enough pictures to give a pretty good flavour of the whole system.

Most of the pictures show appealing little locomotives and four wheeled coaches, trundling through attractive countryside at slow speed on grass covered tracks, but this is a deceptive image….the tramways had some very impressive engineering and a large station at le Mans that was the equal of anything on a standard gauge route. When it was built the network was an efficient, well planned transport system performing a vital role in opening up the rural areas...no one could have foreseen the dramatic changes that the post World War One period would bring.

4059. FILLÉ (Sarthe) — La Gare du Tramways

Some of the civil engineering was cutting edge, with eminent engineers including Gustave Eiffel and Louis Harel de la Noe being employed and happily one major viaduct still survives as described later.

Le Mans lies close to the centre of the Sarthe department so it was ideally placed to form the hub of the system, all the routes radiating out like spokes on a wheel and in may cases making a close connection with standard gauge routes at the terminus.

The tramways system came to an end in 1949, having struggled through World War Two, and much has been lost including most of the architecture but three of the iconic Blanc Misseron Bicabine locomotives have survived to be restored to running order along with a train of coaches, giving us an impression of how attractive and colourful this system must have been in it's heyday.

THE TRAMWAY SYSTEM

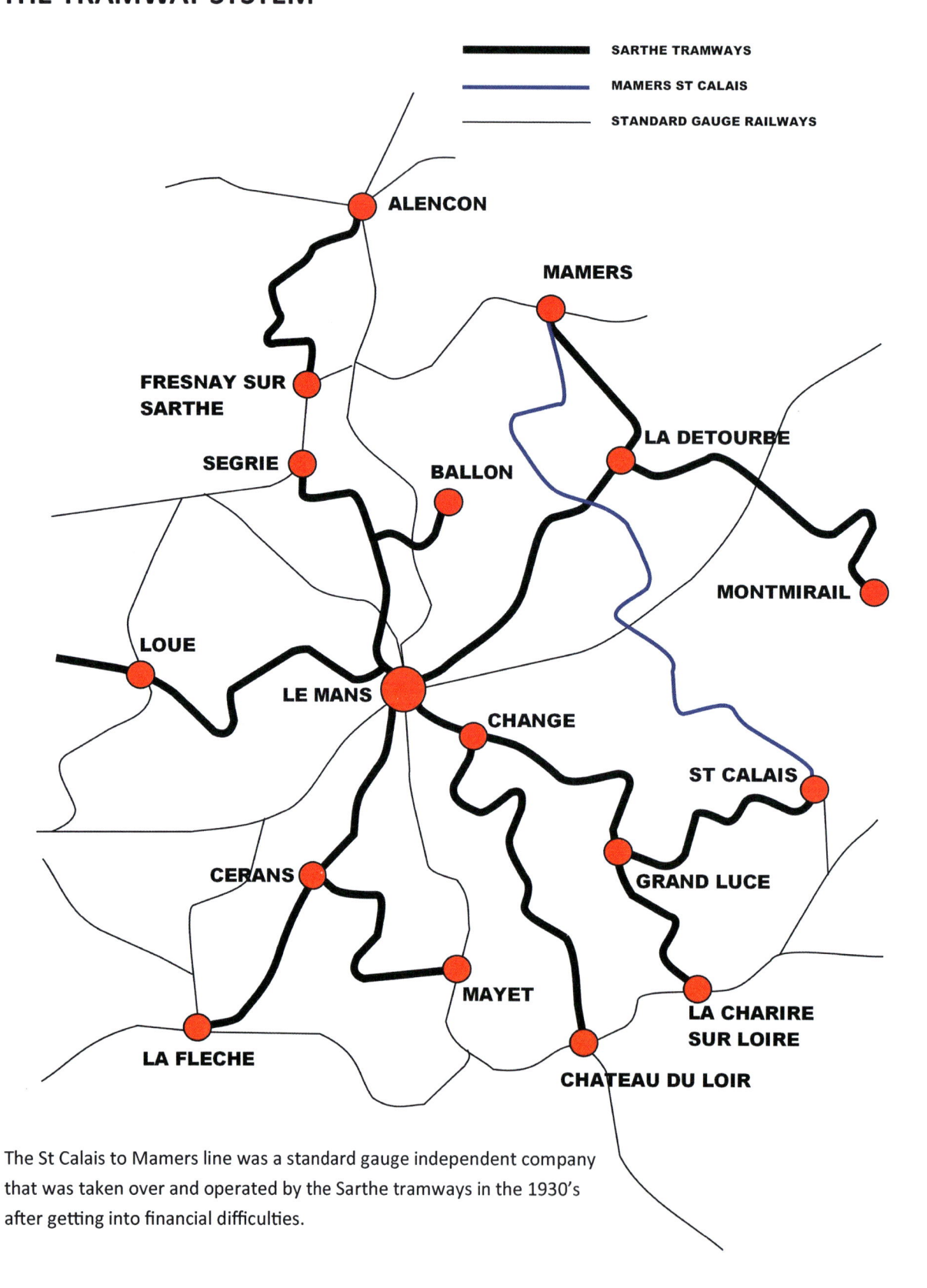

— SARTHE TRAMWAYS
— MAMERS ST CALAIS
— STANDARD GAUGE RAILWAYS

The St Calais to Mamers line was a standard gauge independent company that was taken over and operated by the Sarthe tramways in the 1930's after getting into financial difficulties.

THE SARTHE DEPARTMENT.

The Sarthe department of France, number 72, is like many other named after the major river that runs through it. It was created following the French revolution, the area having formerly been part of the province of Maine. This was split in two, creating the Sarthe and Mayenne departments, in 1790. The major city in the department is le Mans, originally a Roman settlement with some Roman antiquities still remaining.

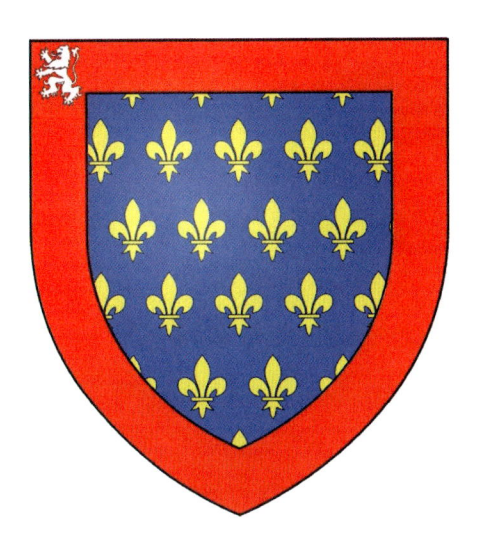

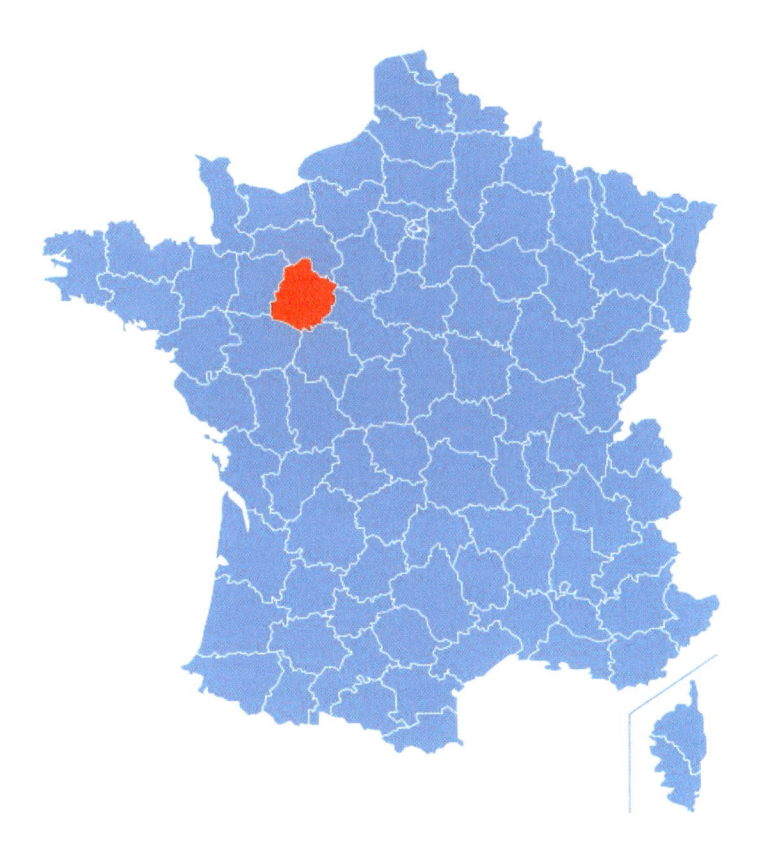

Sarthe lies at the northern edge of the Pays de Loire region and is very much a rural area, half the population living in le Mans itself….there are few other towns of any size. The first railway crossed the department in 1854, but large areas remained untouched once the standard gauge network had been completed which is why the tramway system came into being. Only three towns other than le Mans have more than 10,000 inhabitants but the rural areas are dotted with numerous villages all of which needed an outlet for agricultural produce.

Much of the department is forested, though less so than was the case a hundred years ago, with timber products an important traffic for the tramways. It is crossed by numerous rivers, almost all of which run south to drain into the Loire which runs along the southern border. These have carved deep valleys in places which posed a challenge for the engineers building the tramways resulting in three large and impressive viaducts.

The Sarthe department is not well known in the UK, though most people have heard of le Mans if only because of the motor racing. It is a place worth lingering over, though, largely unspoiled and with beautiful rolling countryside and attractive villages. I hope the pictures in this book will show how appealing it is, and how much more so it must have been when the narrow gauge trains were part of the landscape.

THE STANDARD GAUGE NETWORK.

Before moving on to describe the tramways in detail, it is worth spending a short time looking at the how the standard gauge railways developed as these would create the backdrop for the development of the narrow gauge system.

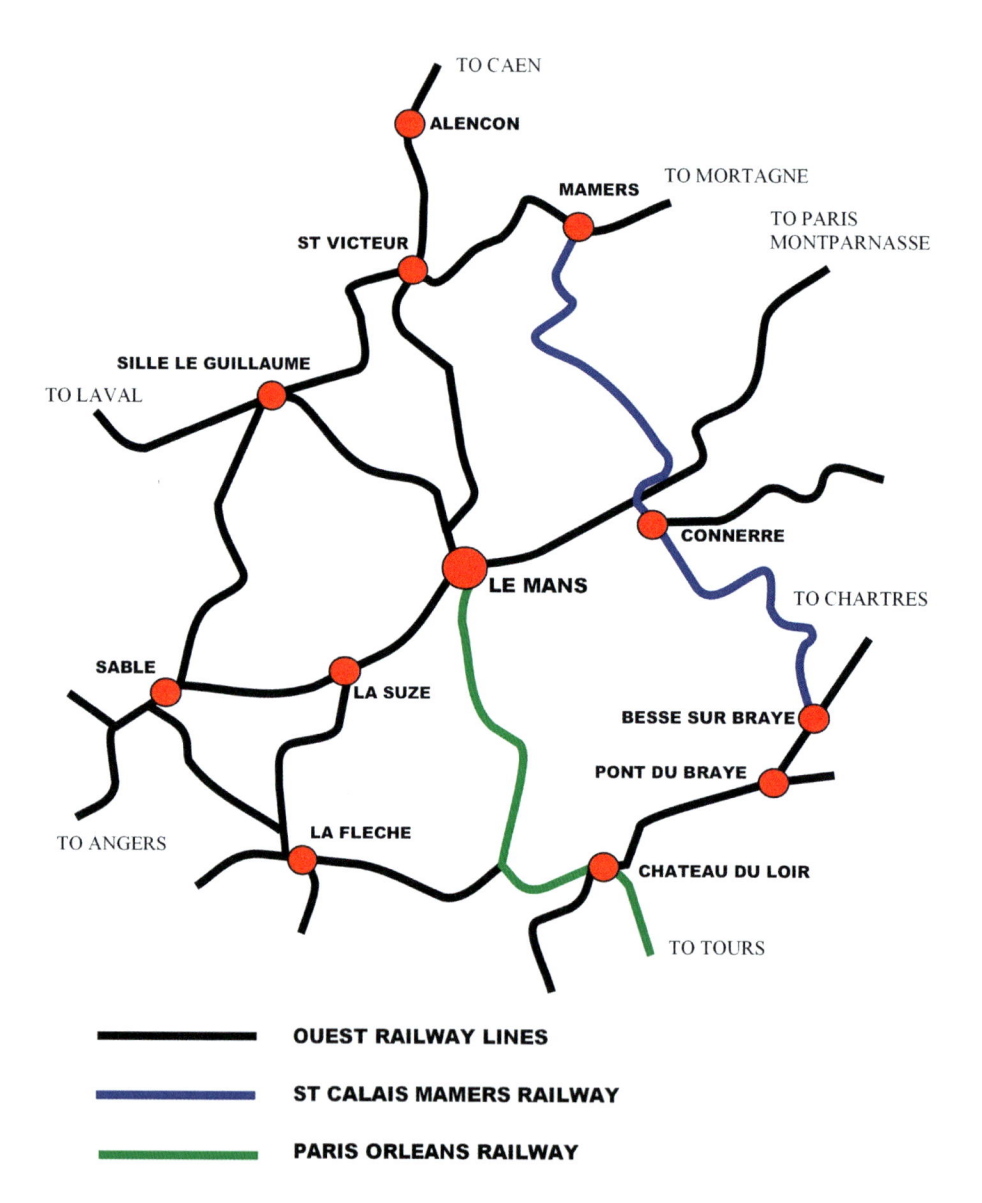

The lines in the department were dominated by the Ouest Railway, which became the Etat and then in 1938 the SNCF....however the lines to Tours was built by the PO company and there was one fascinating independent route, the St Calais and Mamers railway which briefly became a part of the Sarthe tramways network before surviving in part up to the present day as a tourist line.

The first line to cross the department was the Paris Montparnasse to Brest main line, a major trunk route that of course is still open today, though in part supplanted by the TGV Atlantique of the late 1990's. The Ouest Railway main line opened on 1st June 1854, the route continuing west to serve Laval, Rennes and Brest. It was electrified in 1937 from Paris to le Mans, but the war prevented the remainder being converted and this was not done until as late as 1965. The overall roof was removed following the war, and the station has now been extensively modernised.

Between 1937 and 1965 le Mans was the point at which electric locomotives were replaced by steam for the remainder of the journey to Brest.

As with the narrow gauge network, the standard gauge lines radiated out from le Mans as well making it a very busy centre.

LE MANS—LAVAL   Ouest Railway Opened 14th August 1858, and electrified in 1964.

LE MANS—ALENCON   Ouest Railway   Opened 15th March 1856

LE MANS—TOURS Paris Orleans Railway   Opened 19th July 1858

LE MANS—SABLE   Ouest Railway   Opened 23rd March 1863.

These routes all remain open to passenger and freight traffic.

ST CALAIS—MAMERS This was an independent line and remained so when the Etat was created.

>Opened St Calais to Connerre 20th February 1873

>Opened Connerre to Mamers 21st September 1872.

Closed to passengers on 15th September 1965 and to freight on 31st December 1977.

1267. CONNERRÉ-BEILLÉ (Sarthe) — La Gare

THE DEVELOPMENT OF THE TRAMWAY SYSTEM.

The tramways were built in three sections, sensibly spreading the cost and the work of building the lines. The first section comprised just two routes:

Antoigne to Montbizot was the first to open on 6th February 1882.

Le Mans to Grand Luce opened on 26th May 1882.

The first of these lines was a short branch which would remain isolated from the rest of the system until the second group of routes was opened. However it did connect with a standard gauge line at Montbizot. The engineer for both lines was M. Falies, permission having been granted to begin work on March 6th 1880. Once these routes were opened work began on:

Le Grand Luce to La Chartre sur le Loir which was opened on 1st May 1884.

Montbizot to Ballon opened on 17th April 1886.

Le Mans to Loue opened on 6th September 1888

Loue to St Denis d'Orques opened on 6th September 1888.

All the lines were metre gauge and ran along existing roads where at all possible to minimise costs.

In 1893 construction began on the second network, which would total an impressive 257km of route:

Le Mans to Bonnetable opened on 6th May 1897.

Le Mans to Cerans, Foulletourte and Mansigne, opened on 13th September 1897.

Bonnetable to Mamers, opened on 15th June 1898.

La Detourbe to La Ferte Bernard, opened on 15th June 1898.

Once these were complete there was an interconnecting network of lines converging on le Mans.

In 1908 work began on enlarging the system with a third network of routes, some of which remained unfinished when war broke out in 1914. Progress was slower, the first line not opening until 1913 and others not until hostilities had ceased. The finished parts of the network totalled 416km in 1914.

Change to Brette opened on 26th May 1913. **Brette to Marigne** opened on the same day.

La Grand Luce to Saint Calais opened on 6th September 1913.

Foulletourte to La Fleche (Ville) opened on 27th June 1914.

Fresnay to Alencon opened on 16th July 1914, isolated from the remainder of the system.

Le Mans to St Jean d'Asse, opening on 14th August 1915 and finally connecting the Ballon line to the rest of the network. **St Jean L'Asse to Segrie** opened on the same day.

La Ferte Bernard to Montmirail opened on 16th March 1916.

Antoigne to St Jean d'Asse opened on 6th November 1919.

Marigne to Jupilles opened on 26th February 1920.

La Fleche Ville to La Fleche PO station opened on 5th September 1921.

Jupilles to Chateau du Loir opened on 26th June 1922, the last line to be completed. The first closures came just eleven years later.

Not completed were lines linking **Segrie and Asse le Boisne** and **Mamers and Alencon**.

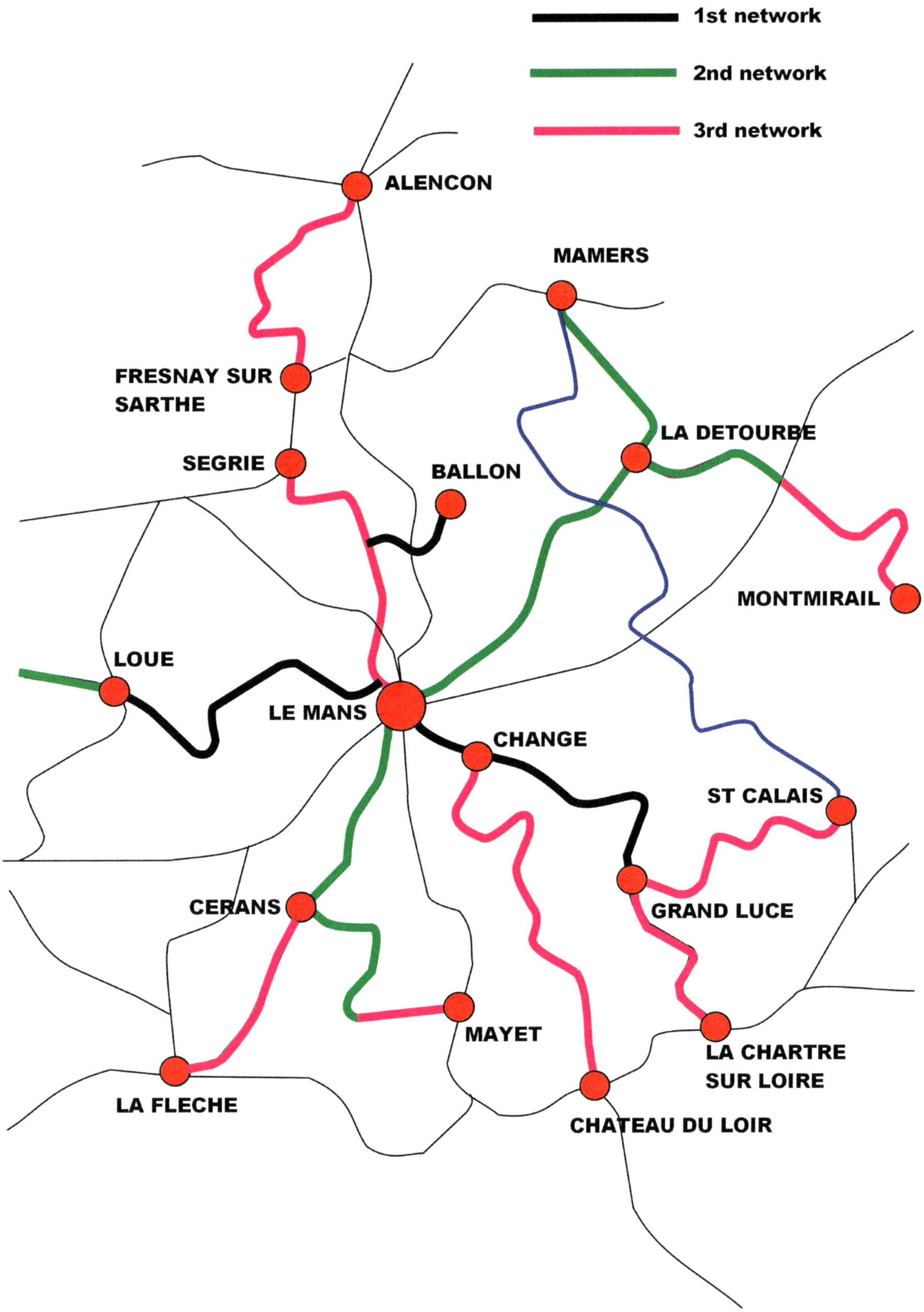
1st network
2nd network
3rd network
ALENCON
MAMERS
FRESNAY SUR SARTHE
LA DETOURBE
SEGRIE
BALLON
MONTMIRAIL
LOUE
LE MANS
CHANGE
ST CALAIS
CERANS
GRAND LUCE
MAYET
LA CHARTRE SUR LOIRE
LA FLECHE
CHATEAU DU LOIR

The development of the tramway network between 1882 and 1922, a forty year period, reflects a well run and carefully planned business. Before 1914 there was little competition and it made sense to expand the system gradually over time, filling in gaps and extending branches. No one in 1910 could have foreseen the changed economic circumstances of the 1920's and 30's which decimated so much of the secondary rail network in France.

It was intended from the start that three return trips would be run daily on each line, though the branch to Ballon only generated sufficient traffic to justify two return workings. The lines from Le Mans to Mamers and La Chartre later had the service increased to four trains each way per day. This is the 1914 timetable:

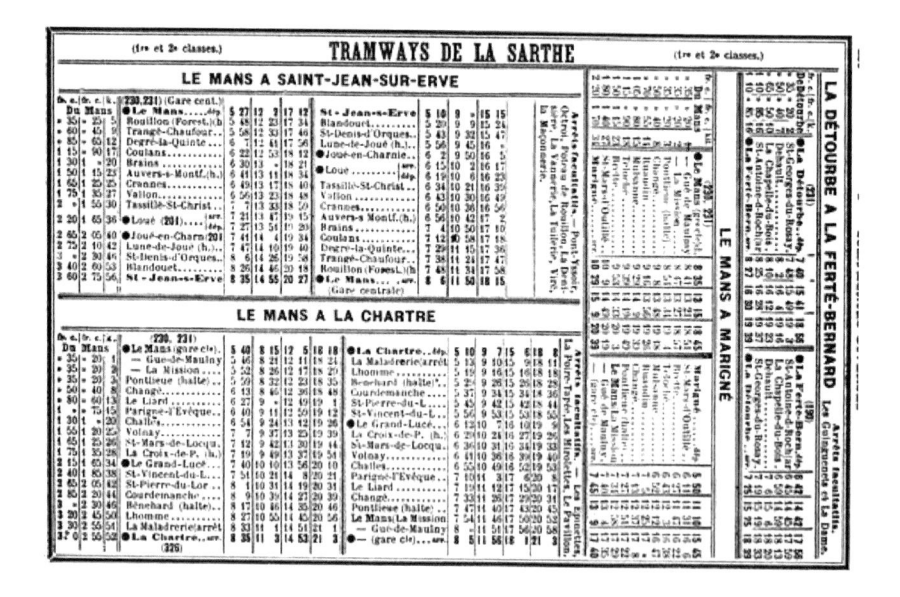

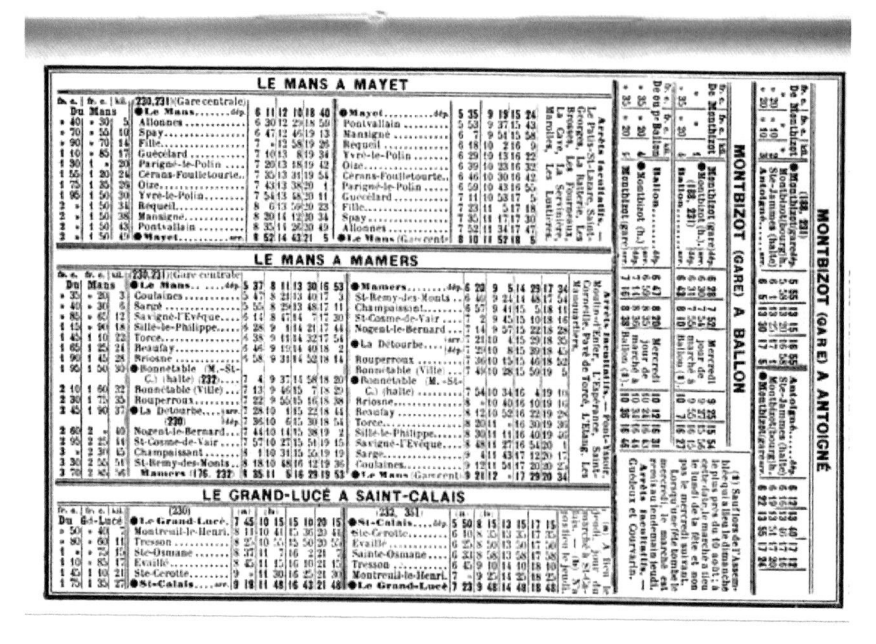

To begin with the 'Compagnie des Tramways de la Sarthe' ran the tramways, but in 1895 this was absorbed into the 'Chemins de fer d'Intérêt Local' though the name Sarthe Tramways was retained.

Remarkably, on 2nd August 1932 the system gained a standard gauge route, the independent St Calais to Mamers railway which was in financial trouble. It ran as part of the tramways company until 1st March 1947 when it was absorbed into the SNCF.

CLOSURE.

Despite being a well run concern the tramways were not immune from the economic realities of the post-war period. Railcars were introduced to reduce costs but to no avail, and gradually the system began to be closed down, the first lines in 1933.

CLOSED IN 1933:

Montbizot to Ballon.

La Detourbe to La Ferte Bernard and Montmirail.

Cerans to la Felche Ville and La Fleche PO. This latter section had only been open for twelve years.

Fresnay to Alencon.

Jupilles to Chateau du Loir.

Mansigne to Mayet.

As was so often the case, generally the last lines to open were the weakest and closed first.

CLOSED IN 1934:

Cerans to Massigne.

St Denis to St Jean sur Erve (closed to passengers in 1921).

Le Grand Luce to St Calais.

Marigne to Jupilles.

St Jean d'Asse to Segrie

Brette to Marigne.

CLOSED IN 1935:

Antoigne to Montbizot abd Antoigne to St Jean Asse.

CLOSED IN 1937:

Le Mans to Loue.

Change to Brette.

Le Mans to St Jean d'Asse.

The remaining lines managed to hang on for a few more years, perhaps due to the war and the lack of fuel for private vehicles. The end was inevitable, though, especially after bombing severely damaged Le Mans station and the workshops.

CLOSED IN 1946

Le Mans to Cerans.

CLOSED IN 1947.

Le Mans to Grand Luce and le Chartre.

Le Mans to Bonnetable and Mamers.

The company was officially wound up in 1949 and the Sarthe Tramways ceased to exist.

Trains passing at Guecelard station on the line to La Fleche, a scene typical of the tramways before 1914.

CLOSURES IN THE 1930'S

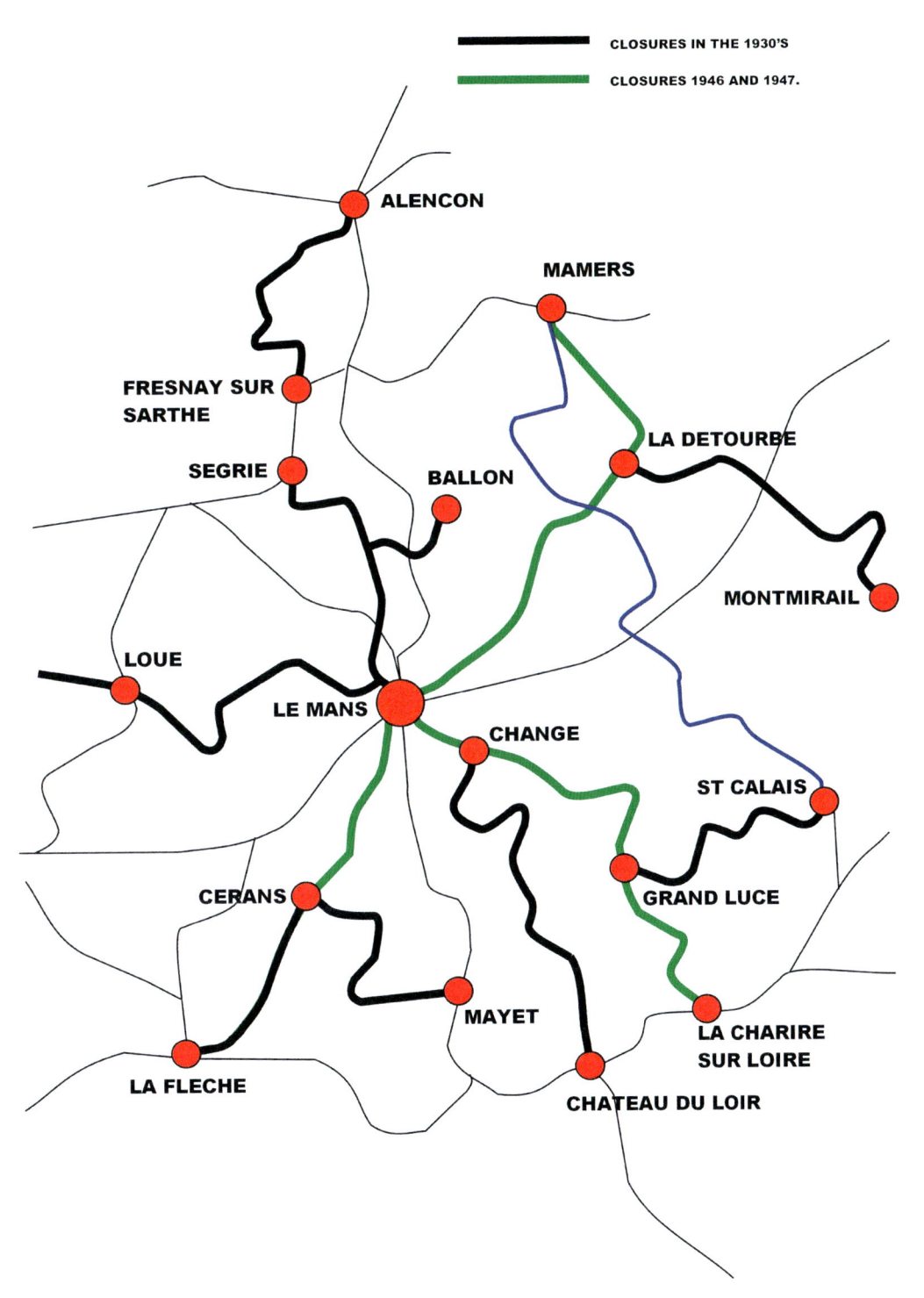

CLOSURES 1946 AND 1947.

As the network began to contract from 1933 onwards it became self perpetuating as with fewer lines there was less traffic feeding into Le Mans which reduced possibility of raising income. Had the war not intervened it is probable that the whole system would have closed by the end of the 1930's, it was simply impossible to compete with road transport.

LOCOMOTIVES AND ROLLING STOCK.

The first lines to open in the 1880s were operated using three different types of locomotives, four 020 (0-4-0T) Corpet Louvet tanks, three Tubize Bicabines and five Blanc Misserons. It seems probable that the company wanted to evaluate the different types before placing a large order. :

1881 : 020T Corpet-Louvet, 1 to 4 (builders numbers 341-44), 6 tons.

1882 : 030T Tubize, 12 (builders number 533), 11 tons.

1883 : 030T Tubize, 13 (builders number 537), 11 tons.

1884 : 030T Tubize, 14 (builders number 540), 11 tons.

1887 : 030T Blanc-Misseron, 15 (builders number 626-1), 16 (builders numbers 681-19), 11 tons.

1888 : 030T Blanc-Misseron, 17 (builders number 682-20), 18-19 (builders numbers 689-90), 11 tons.

For the second network of lines the following were ordered, drawing on the experience gained with the first engines; clearly the Blanc Misseron engines had performed the best, and these Bicabines became the loco's most associated with the Sarthe tramways.

1896 : 030T Blanc-Misseron, 50-54, (builders numbers 1049-54),12.8 tons.

1897 : 030T Blanc-Misseron, 55-58, (builders numbers 1055-57),12.8 tons.

1898 : 030T Blanc-Misseron, 59-61, (builders numbers 1058-60),12.8 tons.

1898 : 030T Blanc-Misseron, 62, (builders number 1061), 13.2 tons.

Finally another batch of Blanc Misseron engines were ordered from 1910 for the newly opening lines.

1910 : 030T ANF Blanc-Misseron, 101-104, (builders numbers 1636-39),13 tons.

1913 : 030T ANF Blanc-Misseron, 105-106, (builders numbers 1737-38),13 tons.

1912 : 030T ANF Blanc-Misseron, 107-116, (builders numbers 1642-52),13 tons.

One of the 1912 Blanc Misseron loco's which after that date worked services alongside the Bicabines; the early batches of engines were pretty much worn out and withdrawn by this time so the replacements were sorely needed.

This example, no. 108, is gleaming so it is probably fairly new; it was one of the next to last batch to be built, no new steam engines being required after 1913. Beneath the side sheets it is a very conventional 0-6-0T loco, more powerful than the Bicabines and ideal for the tramways.

AUTORAILS

In an attempt to reduce running costs, a fleet of railcars were purchased from 1924 onwards.

No 201-202, De Dion-Bouton, type JM2 bought in 1924

No 203, Saurer, date uncertain.

No 204-206, De Dion-Bouton type JM4, bought from the Tramways de l'Ain in 1932.

No 207, SCF.Verney, bought from the Tarn tramways in 1934, type SCF 51—it was transferred in 1945 to the PO-Corrèze railway.

No 207, De Dion-Bouton type JM4, bought from the Chemins de fer des Côtes-du-Nord in 1932.

No 208-212, De Dion-Bouton type JM2, bought from the Tramways d'Ille et Vilaine.

Someone was kept busy sourcing second hand railcars available to be purchased!

Theligny was a halt on the line to Montmirail; despite the large group seen here it was one of the earlier closures.

COACHING STOCK.

The coaches used on the tramways were all four wheeled, and were all very similar in appearance. One might have expected general improvement over a forty year period between the first and last lines opening but that doesn't seem to have happened other than the building of eighteen bogie coaches from 1902. Most of the pictures show the four wheeled coaches, not surprisingly.

The first stock was built by Nivelles in 1881 and 1882 ready for the opening of the first routes, with a further batch following in 1884 to 1886 built by Carel & Fouche.

Numbers A1 to A16 were first class coaches.

B1 to B63 were second class coaches, by far the commonest type.

AB1 to AB20 were mixed 1st/2nd class coaches.

BD1 was a mixed second class coach and van.

BP1 to BP20 were second class coaches with a mail compartment.

The first bogie coach was built by Carel & Fouche in 1902, construction continuing until 1909 but there were only eighteen in all.

AB51 to AB54 were 1st/2nd class composite coaches.

B151 to B165 were second class bogie coaches.

The preserved vehicles are a delight on a warm day, but you can understand why by the 1930's people may have been less enthusiastic about them in the winter.

GOODS ROLLING STOCK

The tramway used:

Box vans unbraked K 1 to 45.   Box vans braked Kf 101 to 167.

Open wagons unbraked L1 to 48.   Open wagons braked, Lf 101 to 137.

Flat wagons unbraked, M1 to 77. Flat wagons braked Mf 101 to 180.

Timber tricks, unbraked, MO1 to 16.

Ballast wagons, unbraked MT1 to 27, braked MTf 101 to 118.

Two good views of the rolling stock used on the tramways. The ends of the open wagons support a tarpaulin bar.

CIVIL ENGINEERING.

The majority of the engineering on the line during the nineteenth century was entrusted to Louis Harel de la Noe, who had the happy knack of being able to combine superb engineering with artistic flair.

De la Noe was born in Saint Brieuc on the north coast of Brittany, where he was to produce may wonderful structures for the Cote de Nord narrow gauge system including a station to adorn his home town. He died in 1931 at the age of 79.

De la Noe's work can be recognised at a glance, his designs look like no one else's and the was a pioneer of using concrete in structures. Who else could have designed a narrow gauge railway station that looked like this…..

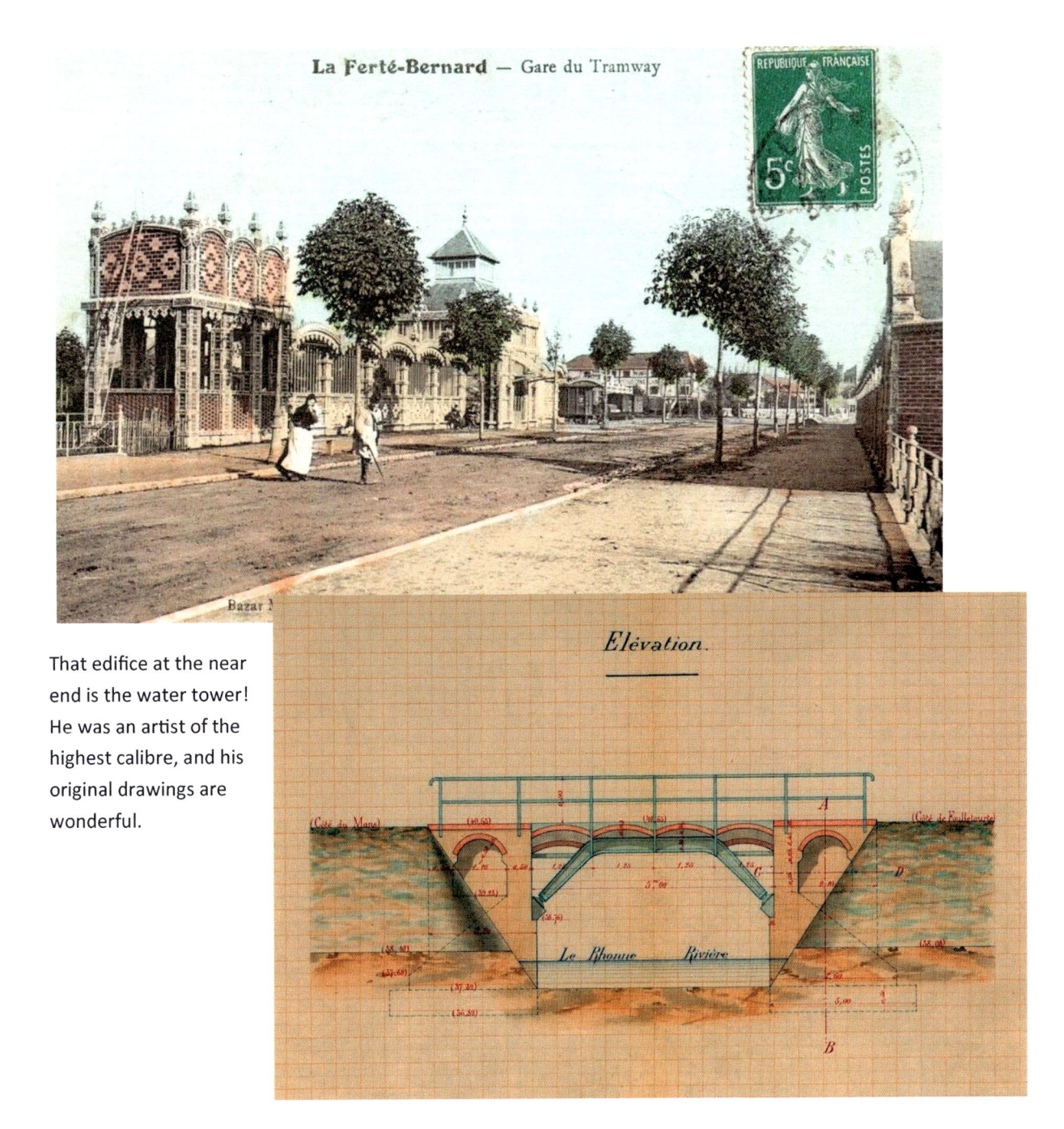

That edifice at the near end is the water tower! He was an artist of the highest calibre, and his original drawings are wonderful.

Noe was responsible for many great bridges and viaducts, but perhaps the most iconic was in le Mans, the famed 'X' bridge. It was built to cross the Sarthe river, and stood next to the road bridge. The shape was to allow two different tramway lines to cross each other, which inconveniently they needed to do right in the middle of the river!

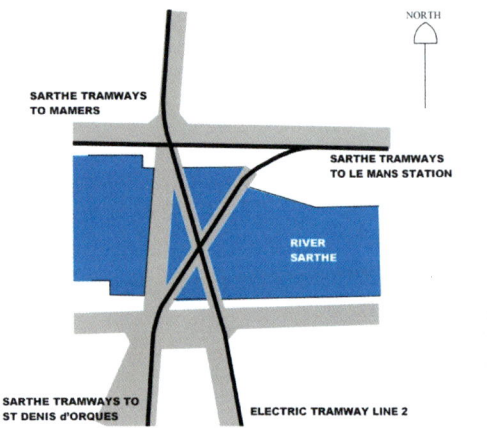

The city had a network of metre gauge electric trams as well as the Sarthe steam powered trains, and this bridge was de la Noe's elegant answer to the problem. Sadly it was blown up by the retreating German army in 1944, a sad loss to the town though one pillar has been pulled from the river and re-erected on the bank as a memorial.

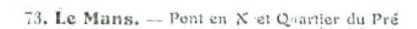

The way de la Noe combined structure with elegance is unsurpassed.

The bridge was opened in 1898, and was awarded a gold medal at the Universal Exhibition of 1900.

This viaduct has all the hallmarks of Louis de la Noe's work.

LOUÉ - Sarthe — Les bords de la Vègre et le Pont du Tramway à la Tuilerie

The metal viaduct on the line to Loue was the work of another eminent engineer, Gustave Eiffel. This was a style he used elsewhere, notably at Mayenne for the tramway there, and it was perfectly suited for the relatively light loads imposed on it by tramway trains.

The line to Loue opened in 1888 which dates the bridge.

This viaduct was not built until 1912 and was destined never to be fully finished but ironically it is the last one to remain standing. The line was proposed to run to Alencon from Maners but was one of the routes that was never finished.

The wonderful viaduct stands 33m tall and is now used by walkers and for bungee jumping. Rather them than me!

The structure is built from concrete, which for 1912 was pretty cutting edge.

THE TRAMWAY ROUTES.

This section describes each of the routes spreading out from le Mans including looking at a selection of stations in detail.

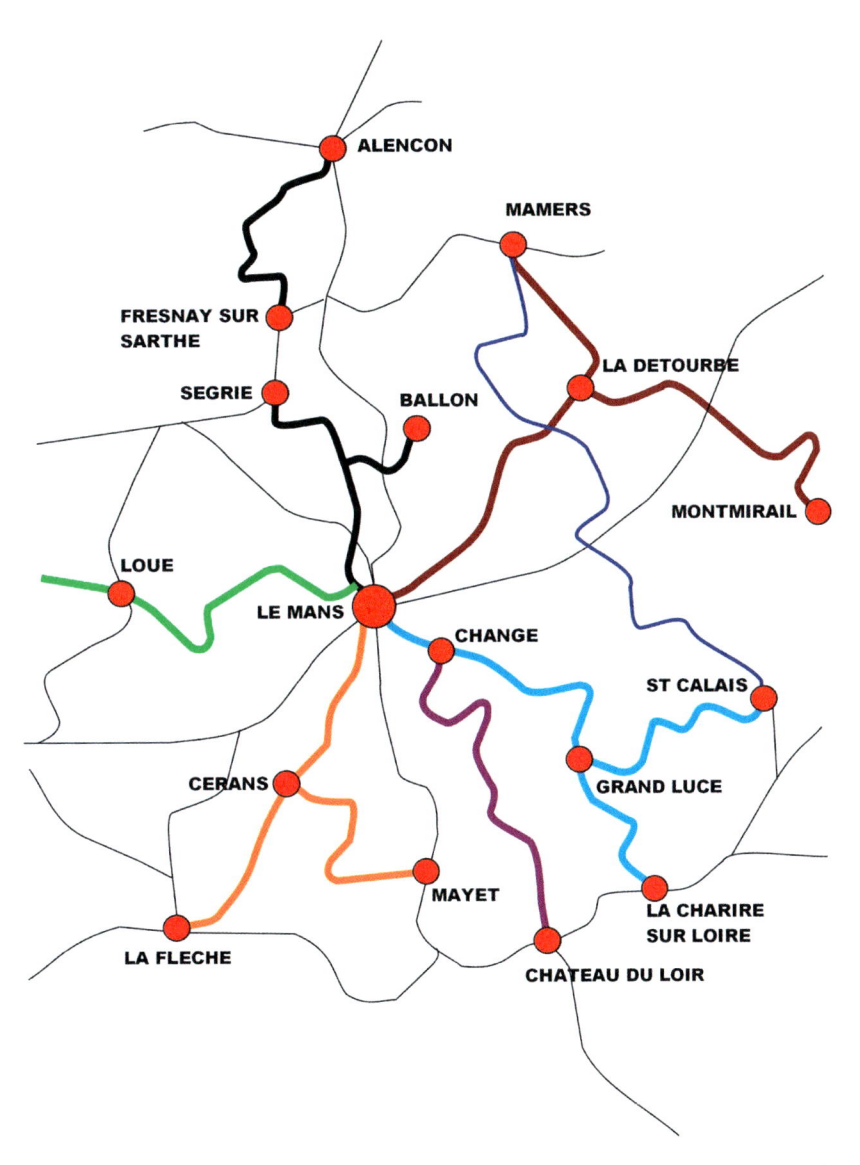

Many of the little stations were never photographed so sadly coverage will be anything but complete but it should be at least possible to give a flavour of each route.

Before heading out into the countryside, though, it seems appropriate to gave a detailed took at le Mans itself.

LE MANS

The hub of the tramway system, le Mans is a large modern city and by far the largest place in the department with almost 150,000 inhabitants. Dating back to Roman times it was the capital of Maine before it was split into two departments, and the name derives from that role.

The large tramway station in le Mans was probably the most impressive narrow gauge station in France, and was the work of Louis Harel de la Noe. It was built on land reclaimed from the River Sarthe in a central position and the various tramways radiated out from it. Add on the city electric tramway, plus the main line railways, and it was a convoluted picture.

A tramway train approaching the station from the south having crossed the river—the station can be glimpsed on the far right. The built up land on the riverbank, held in place with retaining walls, was a feat of engineering in it's own right yet easily overlooked. There were sidings serving the riverside wharves and of course traffic arriving from all the tramway destinations had to be shunted and sorted if it was proceeding beyond le Mans.

137 LE MANS. — La Gare des Tramways de la Sarthe. — LL.

This is the station complex from the road bridge spanning the river; de la Noe's impressive retaining walls show up well with the train shed and station building beyond. Part of the site had been a hospital before the station was built.

A temporary station had originally been opened in 1882 for the first tramway services but the impressive station seen here dates from 1888. It was not greeted with universal acclaim when it was new—de la Noe was mocked as 'Father Nougat' because of his use of different colours in the brick and stonework.

The station was damaged during World War Two and was demolished and the site cleared during 1949.

R. Barbier, édit. — Le Mans.

TO SEGRIE, BALLON AND ST DENIS

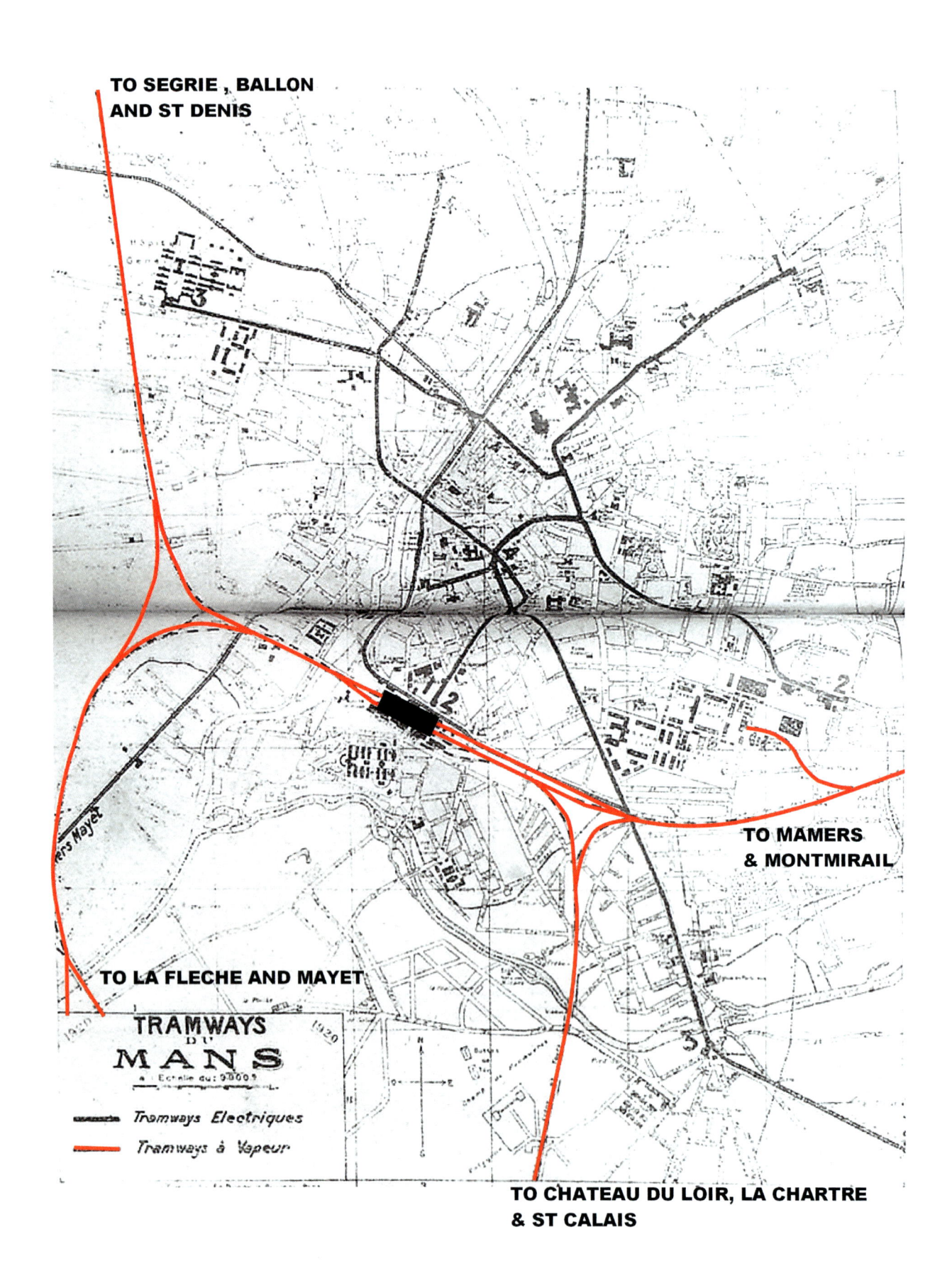

TO MAMERS & MONTMIRAIL

TO LA FLECHE AND MAYET

TRAMWAYS DU MANS

— Tramways Electriques
— Tramways à Vapeur

TO CHATEAU DU LOIR, LA CHARTRE & ST CALAIS

LE MANS STATION 1897 - 1911

LE MANS STATION 1911 - 1949

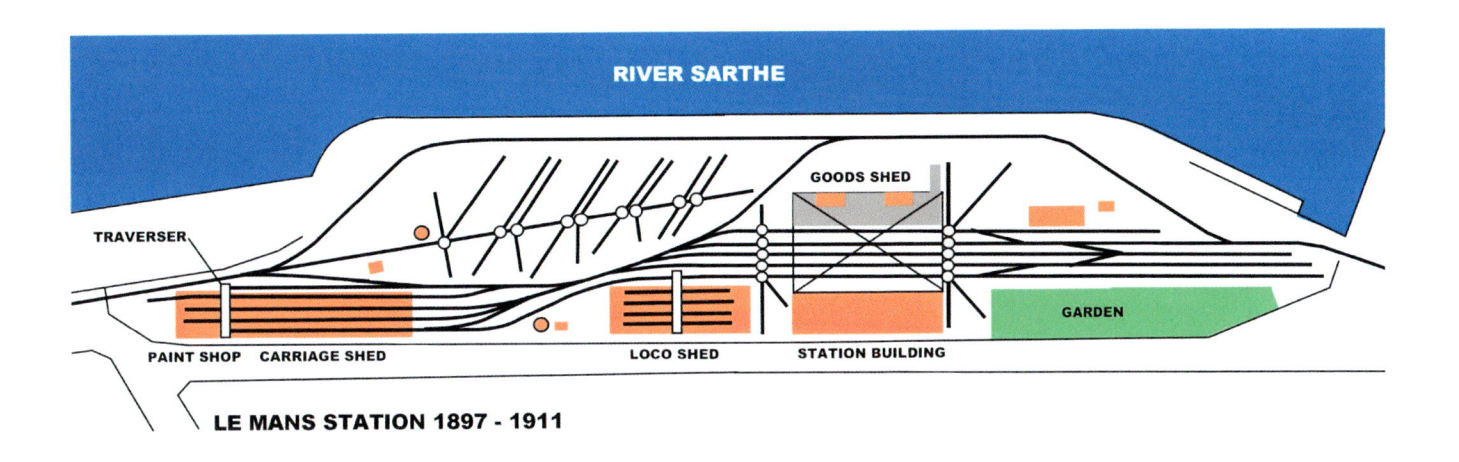

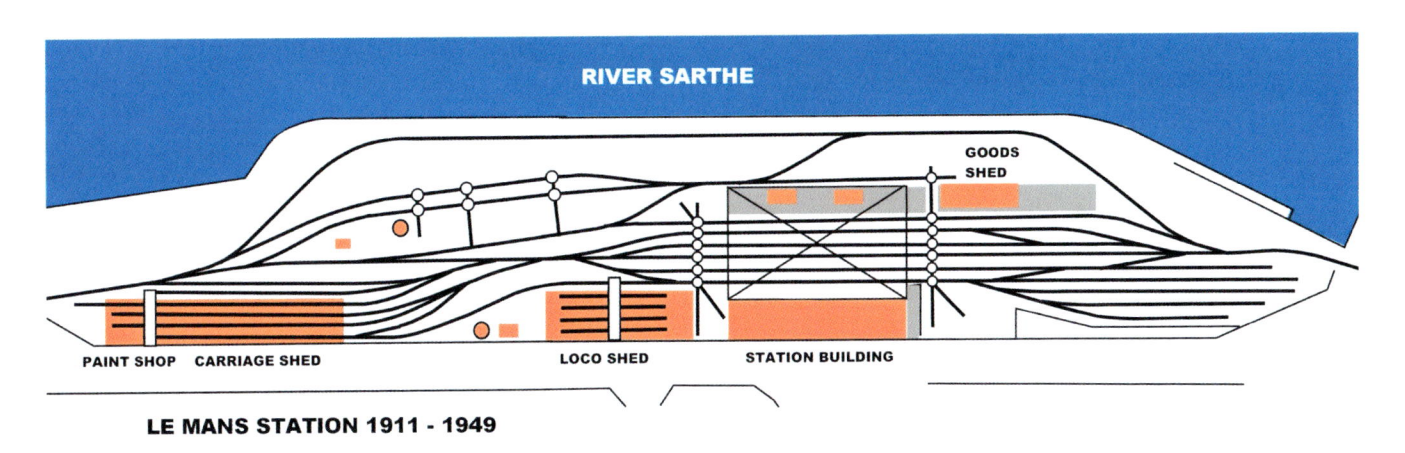

Plans of le Mans station showing the improvements made in 1911 to make working easier. Sadly it would be rather large as the basis for a model railway, and all those wagon turntables would pose a challenge.

One of the 1912 Blanc Misseron engines under the impressive overall roof. The electric light on the loco shows that this is a relatively late picture. It is also one of the best views of the bogie coaches.

A freight train runs through the station behind another of the Blanc Misseron engines, which were a sort of half way house between a conventional loco and a proper tram engine.

Below, the road elevation of the station building, in many ways de la Noe's masterpiece.

La Gare du Tramway — *Le Mans*

The building on the left looks like one of de la Noe's constructions but it was not connected to the tramway, it was a covered market. The station is in the distance.

LE MANS. — Marché Couvert et Gare Centrale des Tramways

Most places would be more than happy with this as their main line station!

La Gare du Tramway de la Sarthe — Le Mans

58 LE MANS. — La Gare des Trams.   R. Barbier, édit. — Le Mans.

The ornate building with the tall chimneys is the loco shed and repair shop, and on the right is the carriage shed.

The river side of the overall roof had a canopy over a goods loading platform.

43. Le Mans. — Gare des Tramways

32. - LE MANS. - Pont du Chemin de fer.
Edition N. G.

32 LE MANS - La Gare des Tramways   L. L. M. - Salle des Dépêches

LE MANS TO LOUE, ST DENIS & ST JEAN SUR ERVE.

The first line to be described ran from Le Mans, initially to Loue where it reversed, and then on to St Denis d'Orgues. This section opened in 1888; it was extended in 1907 to a village in Mayenne called St Jean sur Erve to make a connection with the Mayenne tramways line from Laval. As St Jean only had a population of 650 this was unlikely to be a great success financially and so it proved, the passenger service ending beyond St Denis in 1921.

If through traffic was the goal that was also doomed to disappointment; if you wanted to travel from Laval to Le Mans you wouldn't go by tram, sitting on a hard wooden seat for hours on end at 20kph, you'd catch an express on the main line! Some freight must have been exchanged because St Jean station had quite extensive sidings and the freight trains continued running until the line closed in 1934 beyond St Denis. One does wonder at the rational of building a line like this though, certainly beyond Loue...the traffic potential was minimal. The St Denis to Loue section closed in 1935, and the remainder of the route in 1937.

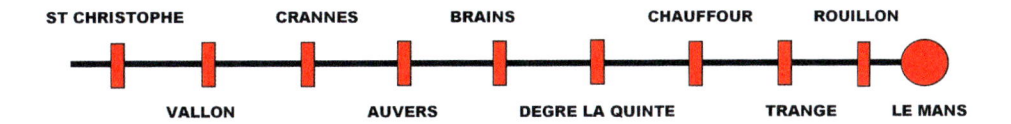

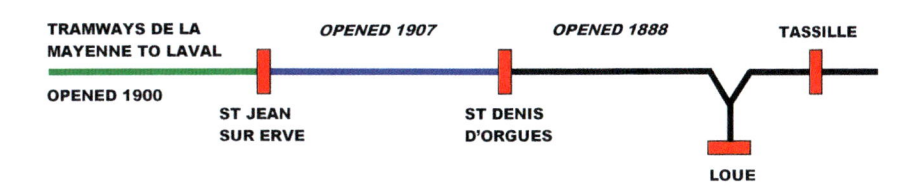

Trange station nestling in the trees; clearly it's a hot day judging by the number of sunshades. This sums up the charm of the narrow gauge tramways.

Degre station, at a slight angle! The station building seems to be a long way back from the track.

Below is Coulans station with the same standard building seen all along this line, including the odd ironwork on the roof.

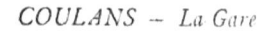

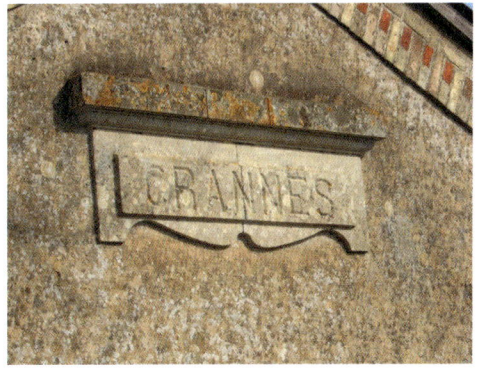

Happily the station building at Crannes still exists in very much original condition giving an excellent impression of how these stations looked. The iron work on the roof, now removed, seems to be supporting a sign of some sort...it would be a very odd place to display the station name.

Vallon (Sarthe). — La Gare

Vallon station—the building is extremely unusual, unlike anything else on the tramway, to the extent that I wondered if it was the correct station but it is. This is a charming picture of a freight train behind one of the Blanc Misseron Bicabines smoking up the countryside.

It looks to me as though the Café was already there and they used it as a station to save the expense of building one. It makes a nice change from the more usual architecture.

Vallon. - Gare du Tramway.

LOUÉ (Sarthe). - La Gare du Tramway

At Loue the tramway terminated alongside the Ouest station on the line between Angers and Alencon. Tramway trains had to reverse before continuing to St Denis. The station at Loue was another that looks very much non standard, but the building in the picture was actually a café.

Loué. - Arrivée du Tramway

Loué (Sarthe) – Gare des Tramways

The station building is the little flat roofed wooden structure, it's little more than a waiting shelter but the design was used quite widely across the system, perhaps where a more substantial building wasn't justified.

The roof of the Ouest station can be seen on the left above the tramway buildings at a higher level.

413 - LOUÉ (Sarthe) – Gare des Tramways

Sarthe. — Loué. — *Gare des tramways à vapeur*

The station basking in the sunshine; it would have been quiet like this for the majority of the time. The approach road can be seen on the right, dropping down from the level of the Ouest station.

Below is the very simple plan of Loue station. The siding served a small brick built goods shed—presumably the wagons were manhandled in and out one at a time.

There was a scheme to extend the line into a loop so that trains could be reversed without running round the loco but nothing came if it; just in terms of the land required it would have been expensive and time wasn't a particularly important consideration.

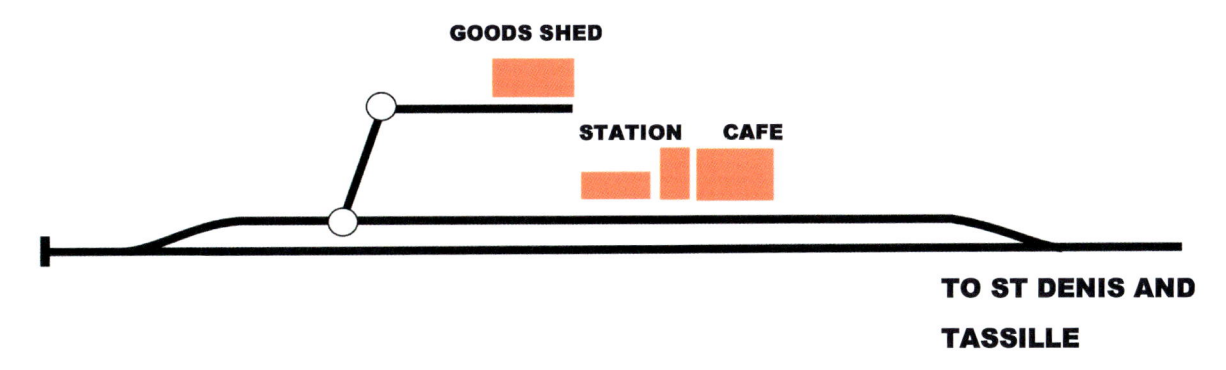

GOODS SHED

STATION **CAFE**

TO ST DENIS AND TASSILLE

The single line split into the two routes half a kilometre beyond the station.

Loue Ouest Railway station with a decidedly mixed local train pulling in. The line opened in 1884 and closed to passengers in 1938 though it is still open for freight.

The station at St Denis d'Orques reverts to the style of those further down the line with the same small station building and that extraordinary metalwork on the roof. This lovely posed picture implies that no train is expected for a while. This was the terminus, believe it or not, from opening in 1888 until the line was extended to St Jean sur Erve in 1907.

It isn't possible to be sure but these pictures probably date from that period. If so, facilities were minimal.

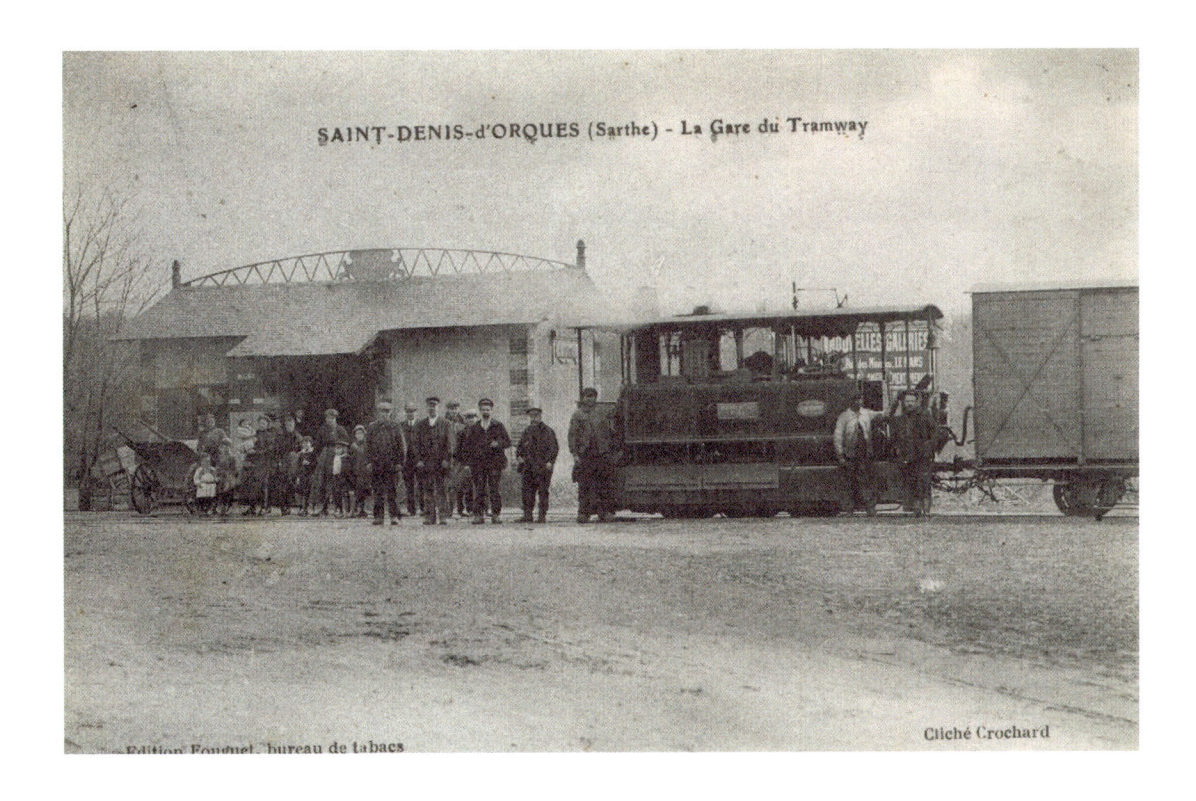

St DENIS-d'ORQUES - Gare des Tramways

This wider view reveals more; there is a small loco shed in the distance and a siding leading from a wagon turntable on the right with a low loading bank.

The loco in the bottom picture seems to be running around it's train in which case the station was probably still a terminus, or looking at the lorry it was more likely to have been taken after 1921 when the passenger service terminated here again. As the population is only 860 today expectations of much traffic could have been misplaced.

St-Denis-d'Orques (Sarthe) — La Gare des Tramways

The line was extended from St Denis to St Jean sur Erve in 1907 to join up with the line of the Mayenne tramways which had opened in 1900.

This plan shows the little terminus before the Sarthe line was built. The population of the village is only 650 which seems to make no sense as the finishing point of a long tramway, but it survived into the 1930's so someone must have been using it.

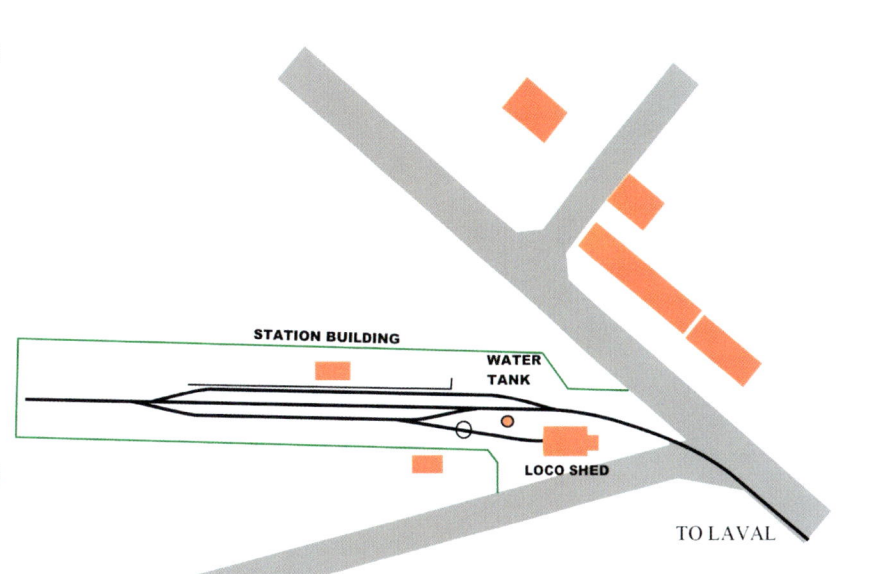

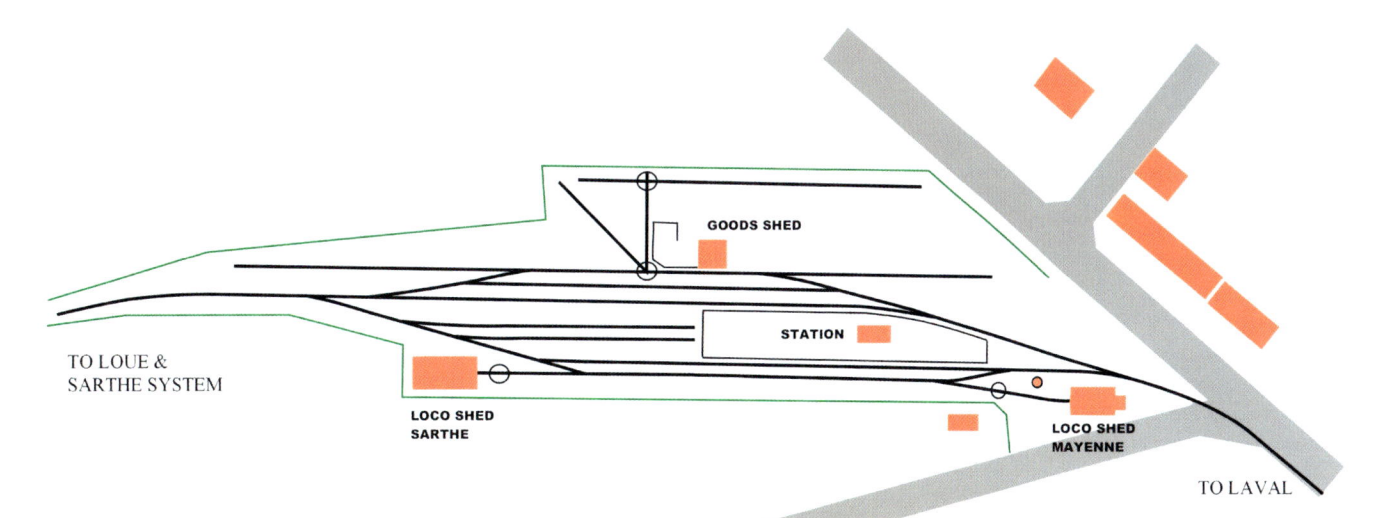

Once the Sarthe line arrived in 1907 things expanded considerably; both lines had their own locomotive shed so that the engine of the last train of the day could be kept here overnight ready for the first departure in the morning. The actual station hasn't changed, with just a little Mayenne building as used all over their system. The building on the left of the picture was a café.

SAINT-JEAN-SUR-ERVE — La Gare

On the right is a loading platform for livestock, perhaps hinting at one of the more lucrative traffics. Far right is the Sarthe engine shed.

Below is the view from the entrance from the road with the Mayenne loco shed on the left. All the pictures show Mayenne trains, unfortunately.

St-JEAN-sur-ERVE (Mayenne) - La gare du tramway

A bright sunny day at St Jean. The track plan looks complicated but the reality was rather flat and lacking in interest. It does not seem to have been a particularly frenetic place!

LE MANS TO LA FLECHE AND MAYET.

The second line in our circular tour (in orange on the map on p29) ran south from le Mans, running to the town of Mayet. A branch left at Cerans Foullertorte and ended at La Fleche adjacent to the PO Railway station there.

The tramway opened in 1897 as far as Mayen, then the branch to La Fleche Ville was opened in 1914, reaching la Fleche Ouest station in 1921.

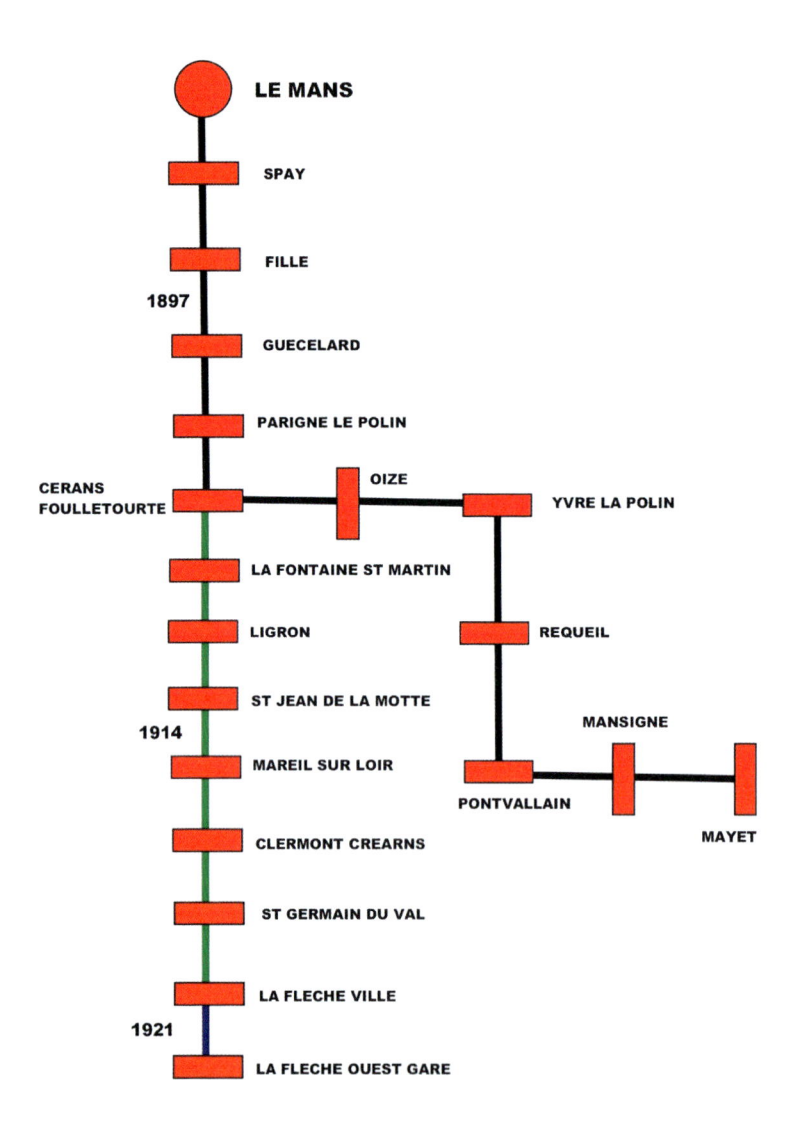

```
                        LE MANS
                          |
                        SPAY
                          |
                        FILLE
              1897        |
                        GUECELARD
                          |
                        PARIGNE LE POLIN
                          |
CERANS                   OIZE
FOULLETOURTE ——————————————————— YVRE LA POLIN
                          |                    |
                        LA FONTAINE ST MARTIN  |
                          |                    |
                        LIGRON              REQUEIL
                          |                    |
                        ST JEAN DE LA MOTTE    |           MANSIGNE
              1914        |                    |
                        MAREIL SUR LOIR        |
                          |                  PONTVALLAIN ——— MANSIGNE ——— MAYET
                        CLERMONT CREARNS
                          |
                        ST GERMAIN DU VAL
                          |
                        LA FLECHE VILLE
              1921        |
                        LA FLECHE OUEST GARE
```

Very few pictures exist of the line between Cerans and la Fleche, mainly because by the time it opened in 1914 the postcard publishers had moved away from subjects such as this. The advent of war must also have been an influence, of course.

Spay (Sarthe). — Café Restaurant Grosbois Dorizon. — Gare Spay.

Spay station, the first stop south of le Mans. The station is a little brick shelter, with the adjacent Café dominating it rather. Most of the stations on this line were little more than roadside halts, the tramway equivalent of the bus stop really.

Below is the view looking in the other direction.

30. - La Sarthe. - SPAY. - La Station des Tramways à Vapeur

Cliché J. Garczynski

FILLE-SUR-SARTHE (Sarthe) — La Gare

Fille station, showing one of the little shelters designed by de la Noe that were used all over the system where a proper building wasn't needed; they may have been made of prefabricated sections. A wagon turntable gives access to the siding on the right, with for some reason a coach standing on it.

Below, one of the 1912 locomotives pauses with a train.

4059. FILLÉ (Sarthe) — La Gare du Tramways

Fillé (Sarthe). — La Gare des Tramways

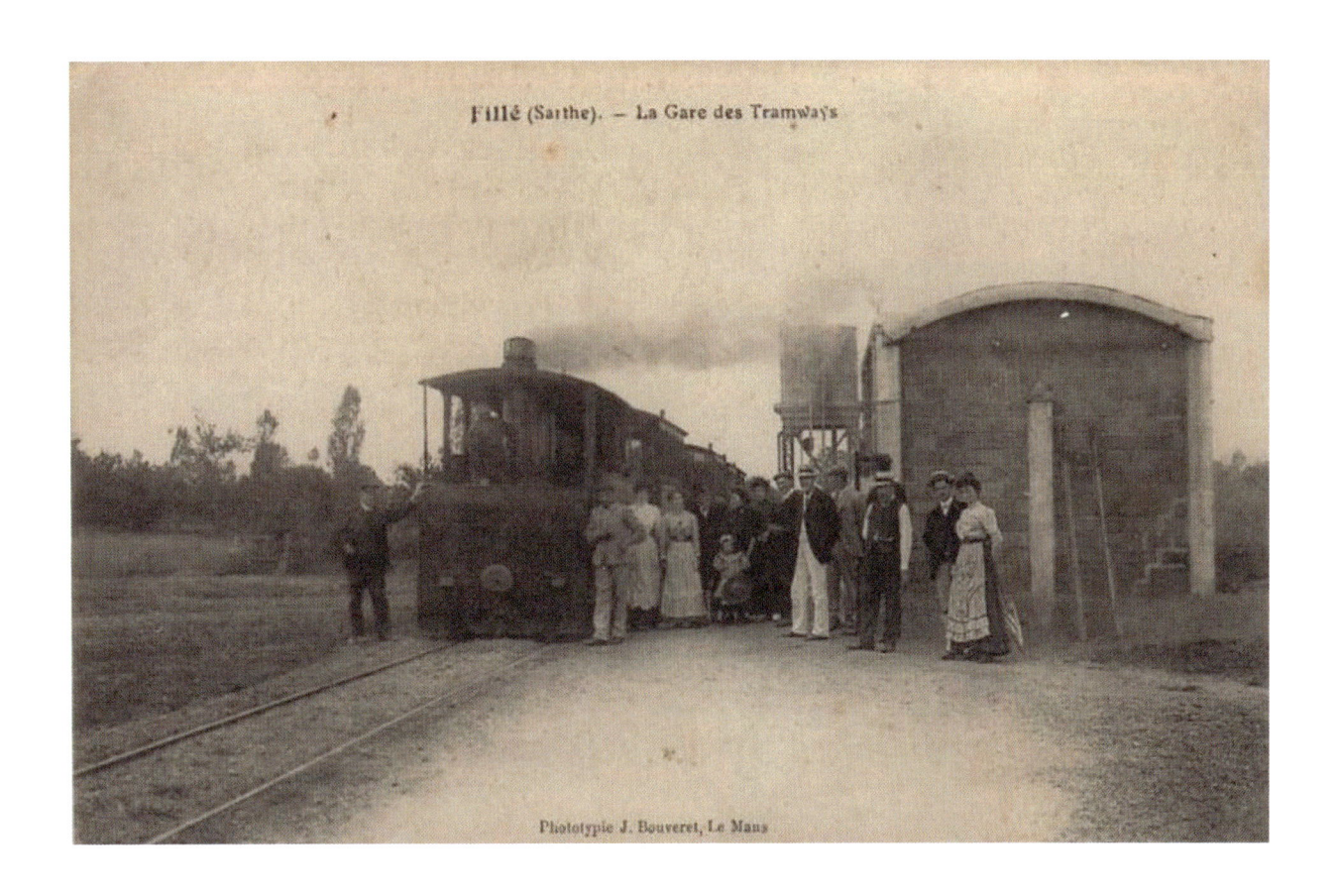

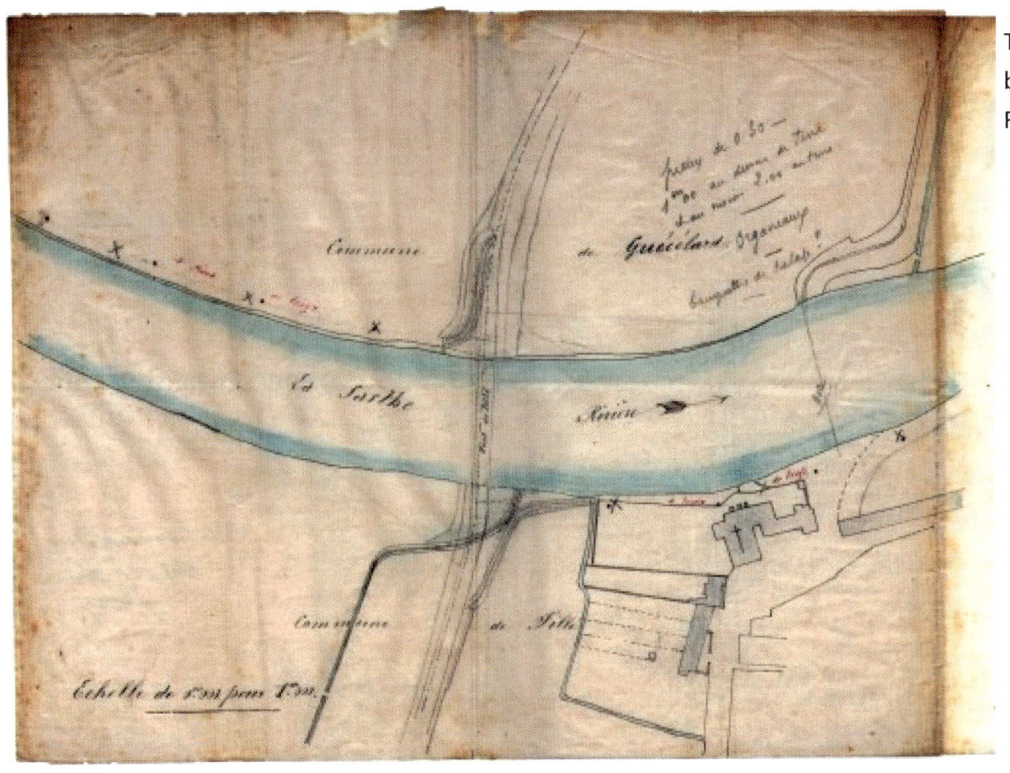

Phototypie J. Bouveret, Le Mans

The plan of the proposed bridge over the Sarthe at Fille.

Trains passing at Guecelard station, a busy scene that would have happened three times each day.

The tramway ran along the unsurfaced road through the village.

GUÉCÉLARD — La Gare des Tramways

There was just a loop here without goods facilities and the building was again one of the small round roofed shelters.

GUÉCÉLARD (Sarthe) — La Gare   21 Janvier 1920

A. Lemaitre, photo. La Suze

A very long train at Parigny station behind one of the 1912 Blanc Misseron engines. The odd shape above the shelter is a poplar tree!

There was a wagon turntable here; an open wagon can be seen on the siding.

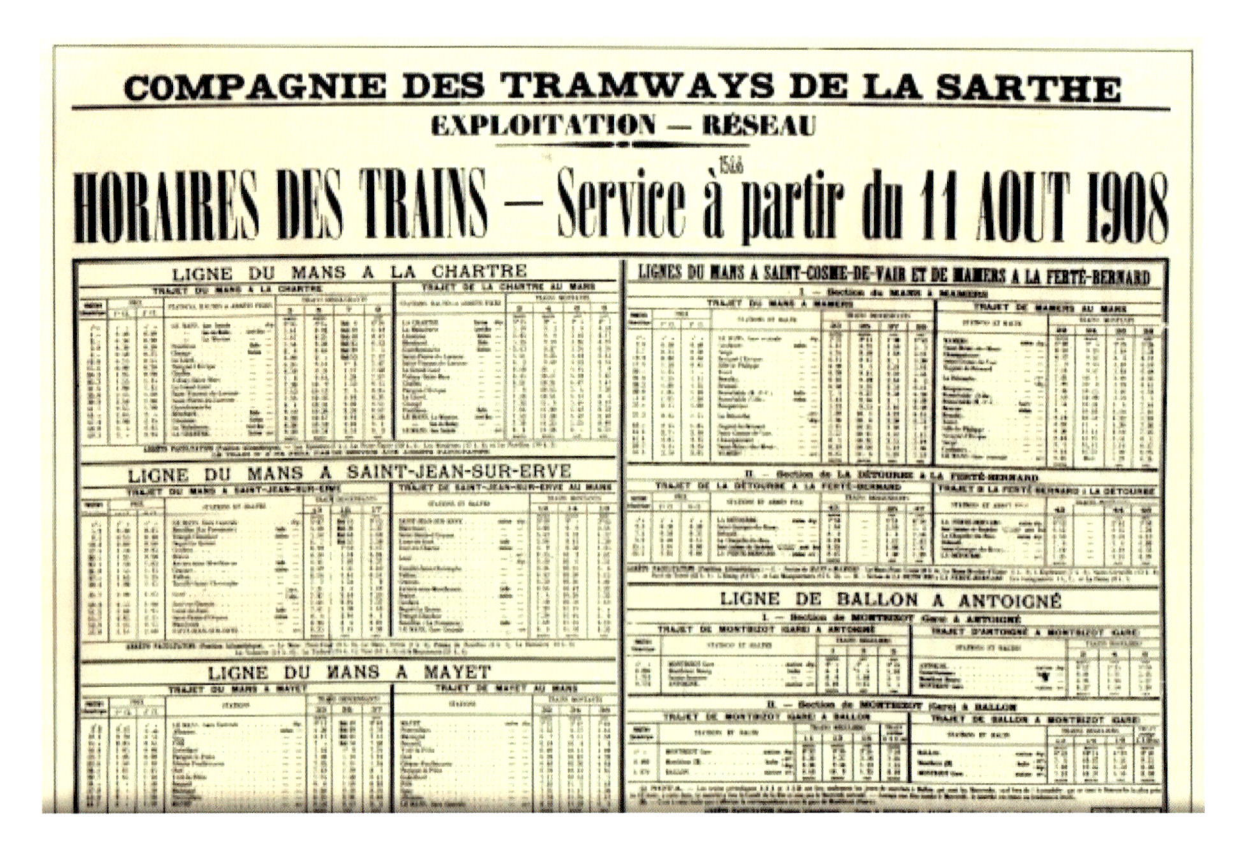

1610. FOULLETOURTE (Sarthe)
Gare des Tramways et Rue Principale

Cerans Foulletourte became a junction when the line to la Fleche was opened in 1914—before that it was just another halt on the line to Mayet.

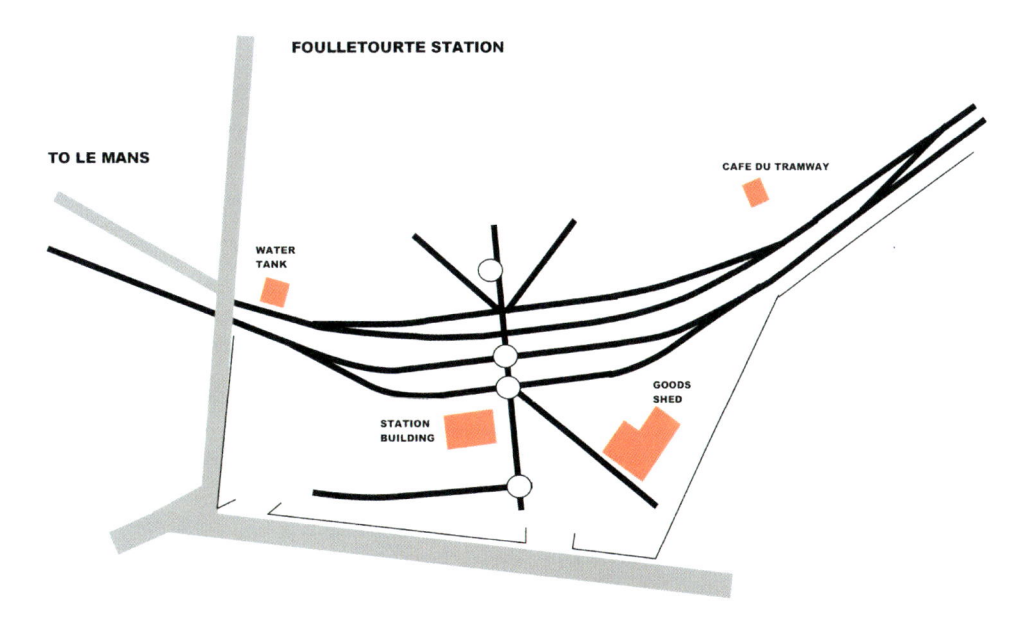

Junction stations are always interesting; here the two routes left the station running parallel for a few hundred metres before separating. The use of wagon turntables was a great space saver in goods yards and the tramway seemed perfectly happy to run trains over them on the running lines.

Foulletourte (Sarthe) — La Gare

The station building was erected in 1914 when the place became a junction and increased in importance.

1523. FOULLETOURTE (Sarthe) - La Gare des Tramways

974. PONTVALLAIN (Sarthe) - La Gare du Tramway

The halt at Pontvallain again followed the standard pattern; there is a turntable on both tracks of the loop connecting to the siding.

Pontvallain. - La Gare des Tramways

MANSIGNÉ (Sarthe) — La Gare

We will continue down the original line to Mayet. This is the station at Mansigne, another of the standard halts used all along this section. The wagons on the lower picture show that there was a siding here accessed from a turntable.

2. MANSIGNÉ — Gare des Tramways

9. MANSIGNÉ (Sarthe) — La Gare

Edit. Brier — Bourdon phot.

MANSIGNÉ (Sarthe) — La Gare

1982. MAYET (Sarthe) — La Gare

Mayet station was on the PO Railway line from le Mans to Tours. The tramway terminated outside the station, unfortunately without being photographed.

344. MAYET (Sarthe) — La Gare

La Flèche. — La Gare, vue intérieure

La Fleche Ouest station was a major junction between four routes but passenger trains finished in 1970 and freight in 1990.

The tramway from Cerans terminated outside the station after 1921, but there seem to be no pictures at all of this section.

40 LA FLÈCHE. — Intérieur de la Gare. — LL.

LE MANS TO CHATEAU DU LOIR, LA CHARTRE SUR LE LOIR AND St CALAIS.

These lines are in purple and light blue on the map on page 29.

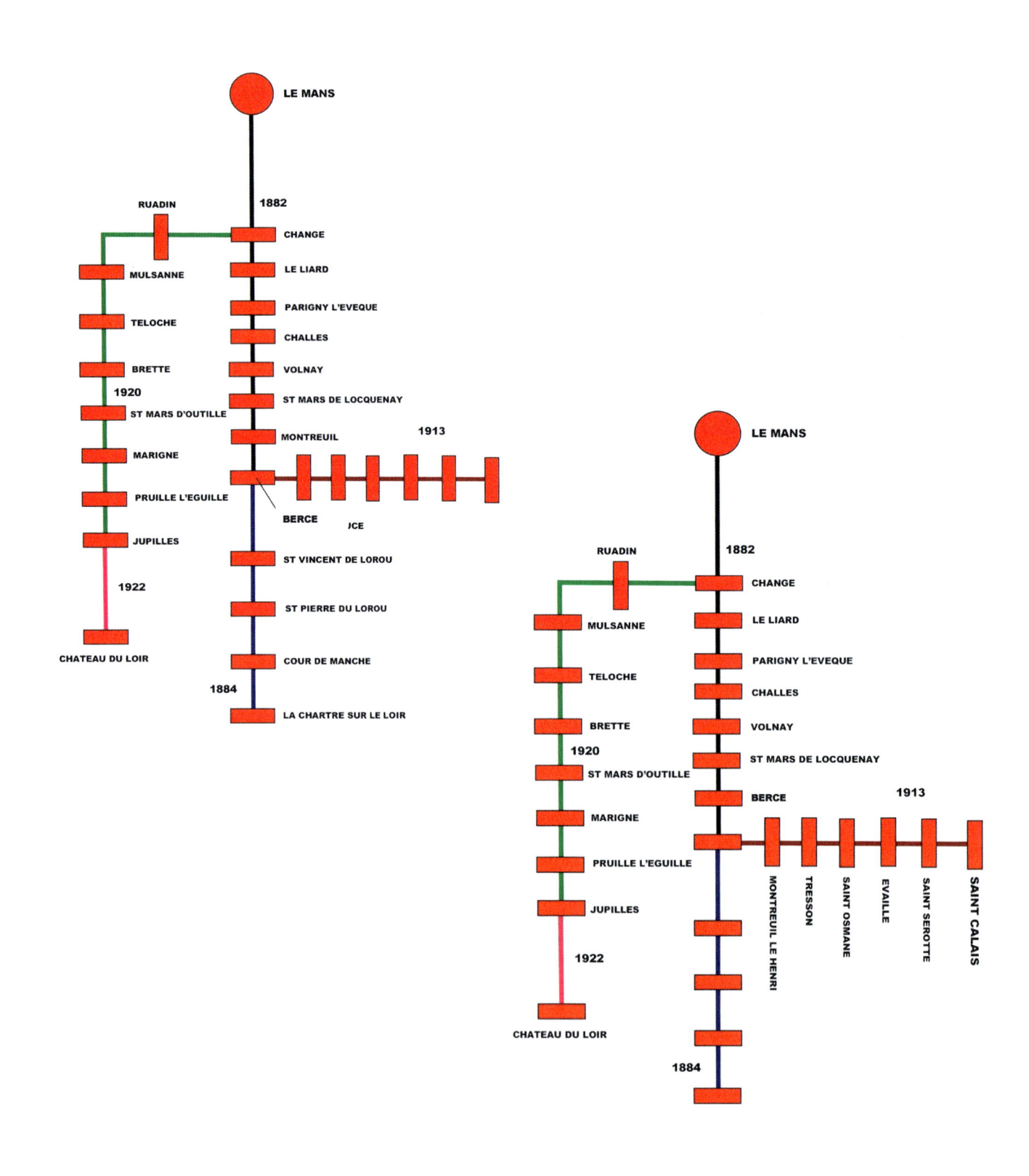

The tramway line running south east from le Mans to La Grand Luce opened in 1882, one of the early lines, and was extended to La Chartre sur le Loir in 1884.

La Sarthe. - CHANGÉ. - Station du Tramway à vapeur à Bois-Martin

This is Change, the first stop after the line ran out of le Mans. The tramway is on the right running along the roadside verge.

Below is Parigny l'Eveque, with one of the wooden buildings already seen at Loue. These have a temporary look about them but don't appear to have been replaced.

20. PARIGNE-L'EVEQUE (Sarthe) — La Gare

This is a brilliant picture, though the fact that the tramway is on it is just by chance.

The lower picture shows that there was a loop with at least one siding running from a turntable. This is a very long train, so traffic must have been pretty healthy when it was taken in about 1920.

Volnay station had one of the attractive brick shelters used on many of the early routes. Timber seems to have been an important traffic, here loaded on ordinary low sided open wagons rather than specialist timber trucks.

All the stations followed the same pattern with the shelter in yellow and red brick with a tiled roof.

The siding is only connected to the loop line by a turntable, seen here in this 1920's picture with a high sided open wagon on the left.

Le Grand Luce was just another roadside halt until it became a junction when the line to Saint Calais was opened in 1913…in this picture from the earlier era some intricate shunting seems to be going on.

Sarthe. — Le Grand-Lucé. — *Gare des Tramways*

Two views of the original station showing that the station building had the decorative ironwork on the roof already seen on the Loue line. Facilities were minimal at that time, the station was no more important than any of the other halts on the route.

Le Grand-Lucé (Sarthe). - Gare des Tramways.

GRAND LUCE STATION

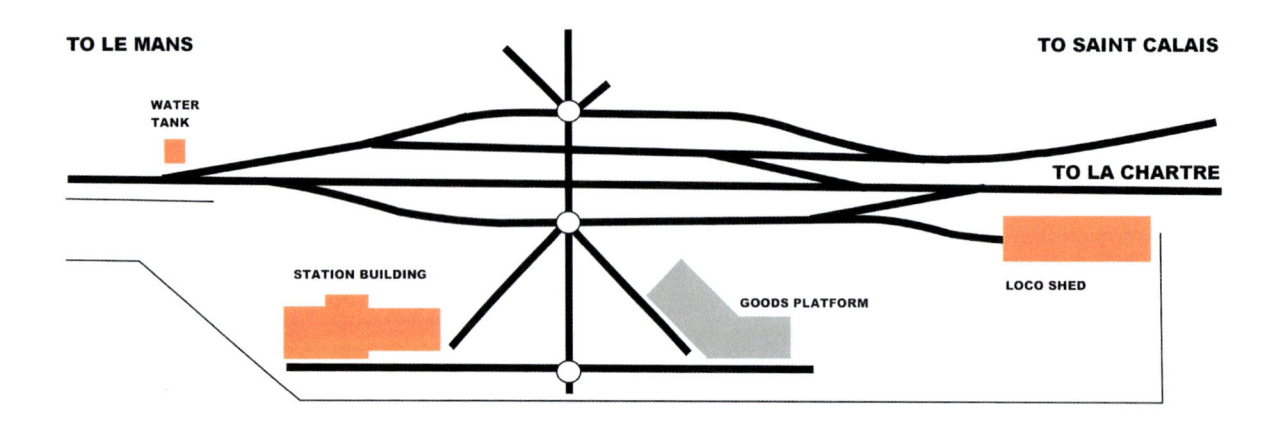

The plan shows the station from 1913 until the lines closed, and includes a single road engine shed which was probably for the loco used on the St Calais branch.

This picture shows the station after it was rebuilt in 1913 as a junction, with stacks of new sleepers in the foreground which were perhaps being used for one of the tramway extensions of the 1920's.

Two pictures of the station after the 1913 rebuilding. Again timber is in evidence, perhaps waiting to be loaded onto the open wagons on the right. None of the stations had a crane so it was all done by muscle power. There is now a goods shed and a siding ran behind it for unloading.

This is the only picture I have of one of the stations between le Grand Luce and la Chartre. Presumably the others were similar—this is St Vincent, with another of the wooden station buildings. I wonder if these were built initially to see if traffic developed enough to justify building something better….seemingly in this case it didn't. There are at least two sidings running from the turntable. Hay is being loaded from a cart onto an open wagon, one of which is already attached to the engine with a tarpaulin over the load in case of sparks landing on it.

LA CHARTRE-SUR-LOIR. — Gare des Tramways

The tramway was opened to this delightful station, called La Chartre Maladerie, on 1st May 1884 and an extension to the main line station followed on 21st September the same year. That wooden building at the near end of the station is another of the shelters similar to the one at St Vincent. Beyond the station building is a goods shed, and a siding runs behind the station on the right.

The station building is unusual, with an external staircase to the upper floor.

La Chartre-sur-Loir (Sarthe). — La Gare des tramways

LA CHARTRE STATION

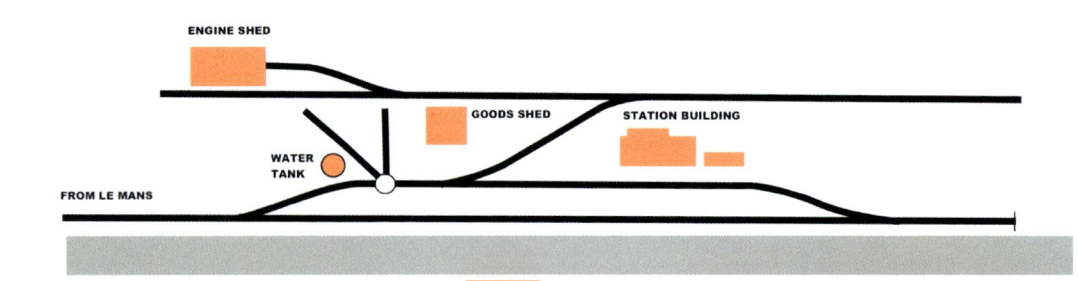

This is the main line station where the tramway terminated, but all the pictures I have show the platform side.

THE BRANCH FROM CHANGE TO CHATEAU DU LOIR.

This branch line of the system left the La Chartre line at Change and ran south to Jupilles and Chateau du Loir. It was one of the last parts of the Sarthe Tramways to be built, in 1920 as far as Jupilles and in 1922 to Chateau du Loir. Just eleven years later it had closed, a reflection of the rapidly changing times.

Due to the short period when the line was in operation pictures are scarce.

1060. SAINT-MARS-D'OUTILLÉ (Sarthe) - La Gare

St Mars typifies the stations, all small halts with a shelter in red and yellow brick with a tiled roof. There is a loop with a siding served from a wagon turntable and that's about it.

MARIGNÉ. - Gare du Tramway

Marigny had a very similar arrangement, which was all the traffic justified. However, the lower card looking the other way shows that unexpectedly there as a loco shed here with a water tank. Marigny station was about half way along the line so it seems an odd place to have the engine shed, especially as there was also one at the terminus.

MARIGNÉ (Sarthe) - La Gare - Arrivée d'un train   Cliché Lelong-Hublin

1764. - MARIGNÉ (Sarthe). - Quartier de la Gare

All the places along the line were villages; Marigne has a population today of only 605 so traffic potential was pretty limited.

Below is the line running into Chateau du Loir, where the tramway terminated...the town is larger with over four and a half thousand people so you can understand the logic of building the line even at such a late date.

516. CHATEAU-du-LOIR (Sarthe) — Square et Château de Riablay

515. CHATEAU-du-LOIR (Sarthe) — Gare des Tramways

This appears to be the only picture that exists of the terminus station at Chateau du Loir, and it shows a very minimal terminus with just the standard brick shelter as a station building. There is a wooden engine shed with a water tank and not a lot more. By 1920 keeping costs down was crucial, not that things had ever been otherwise on the tramways.

CHATEAU DE LOIRE STATION

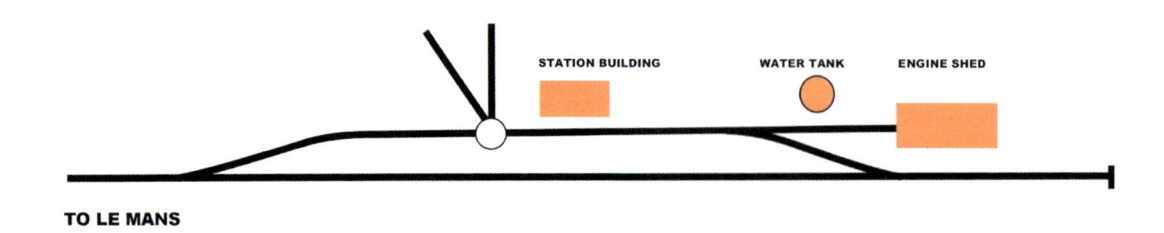

STATION BUILDING — WATER TANK — ENGINE SHED

TO LE MANS

For a minimum space narrow gauge terminus as the basis for a model railway you could do worse, but with the only sidings accessed from a turntable operation would be limited.

THE BRANCH FROM LE GRAND LUCE TO SAINT CALAIS.

The second line to branch off the main tramway ran from Le Grand Luce to Saint Calais and opened in 1913.

Photographs are even thinner on the ground here, unfortunately.

The line under construction at Tresson in about 1912.

This picture of Saint Osmane station will have to do to illustrate the others; they were all similar and followed the pattern we have already seen.

The tramway terminated outside the standard gauge St Calais station of the St Calais and Mamers Railway, a remarkable edifice with the goods shed and station building combined under one roof. There do not seem to be any pictures of the tramway side of things.

LE MANS TO MAMERS, LA FERTE BERNARD AND MONTMIRAIL.

This group of lines were built in stages beginning with the le Mans to Bonnetable section which opened in 1897.

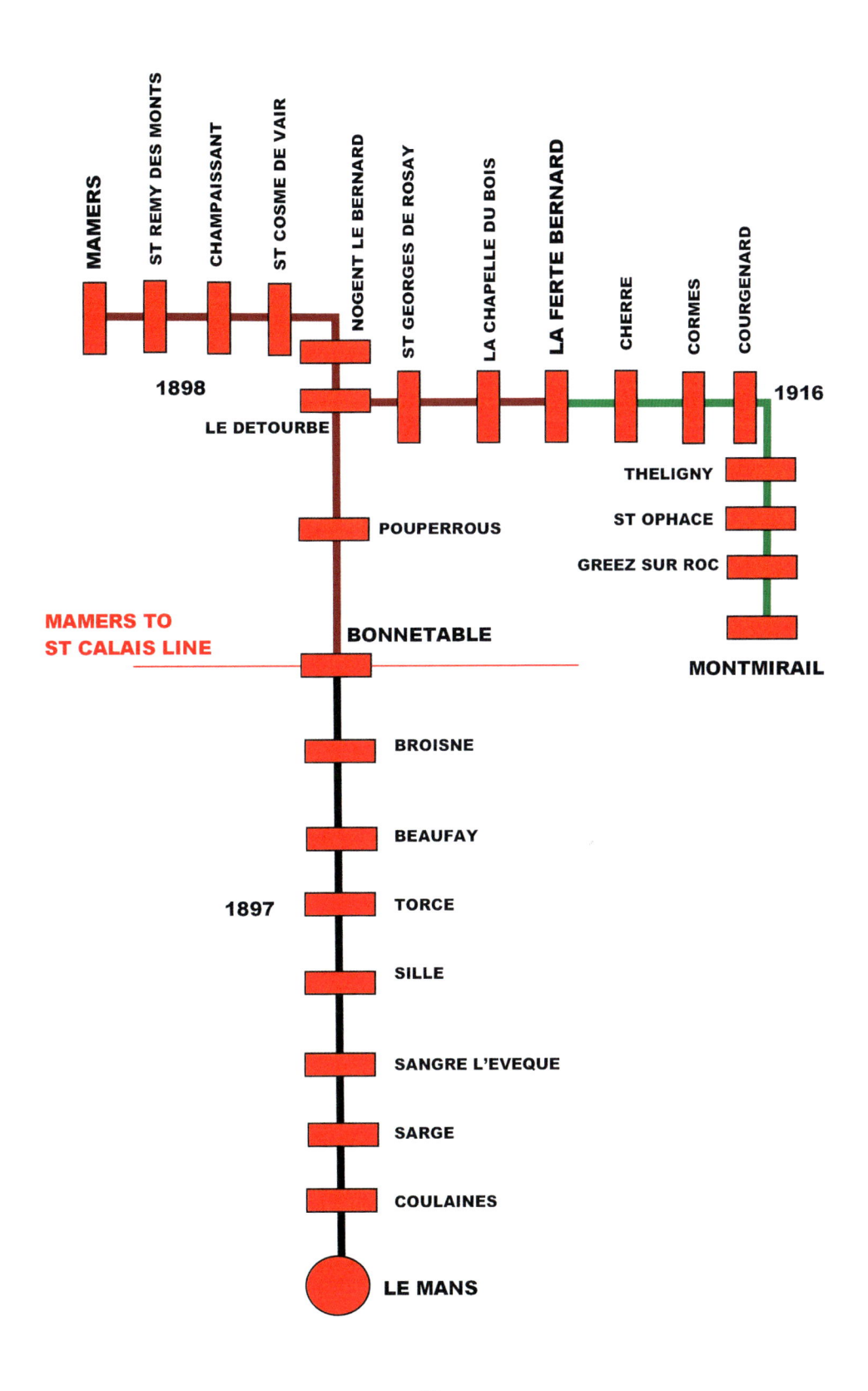

Stations on the 1898 branch (Mamers line): MAMERS – ST REMY DES MONTS – CHAMPAISSANT – ST COSME DE VAIR – NOGENT LE BERNARD – LE DETOURBE

Stations on the La Ferte Bernard line: ST GEORGES DE ROSAY – LA CHAPELLE DU BOIS – LA FERTE BERNARD – CHERRE – CORMES – COURGENARD

1916 branch to Montmirail: THELIGNY – ST OPHACE – GREEZ SUR ROC – MONTMIRAIL

Main line from Le Detourbe south (1897): POUPERROUS – BONNETABLE (MAMERS TO ST CALAIS LINE crosses here) – BROISNE – BEAUFAY – TORCE – SILLE – SANGRE L'EVEQUE – SARGE – COULAINES – LE MANS

83

LE MANS TO BONNETABLE.

This line was built as part of the second network, running north east out of le Mans in a fairly straight line to Bonnetable, where it crossed the standard gauge railway between St Calais and Mamers.

The sun didn't always shine! Coulans station in the rain, showing that on this line the station buildings matched those on the Loue route with brick built shelters with that ironwork on the roof.

The next station of which I have pictures is Bonnetable.

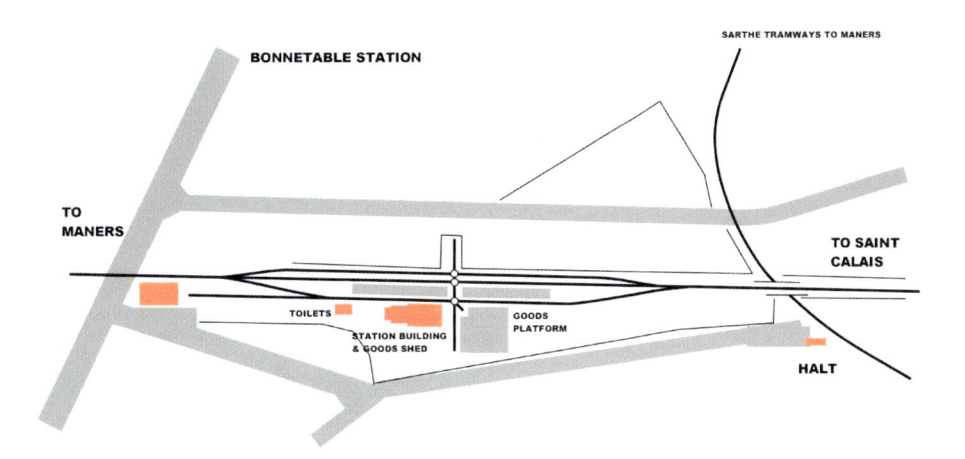

This plan shows the standard gauge station on the St Calais to Mamers line, but the justification is that the tramway crosses the right hand side of the plan, running beneath the standard gauge route and having a halt so that passengers could transfer between the two. The tramway station serving Bonnetable would be reached by following the line off the plan to the top right.

This is Bonnetable tramway station, a significant structure being provided for this market town. On the right is one of the stone shelters we have encountered before, and behind it is a station building identical to the one provided at Chateau de Loir.

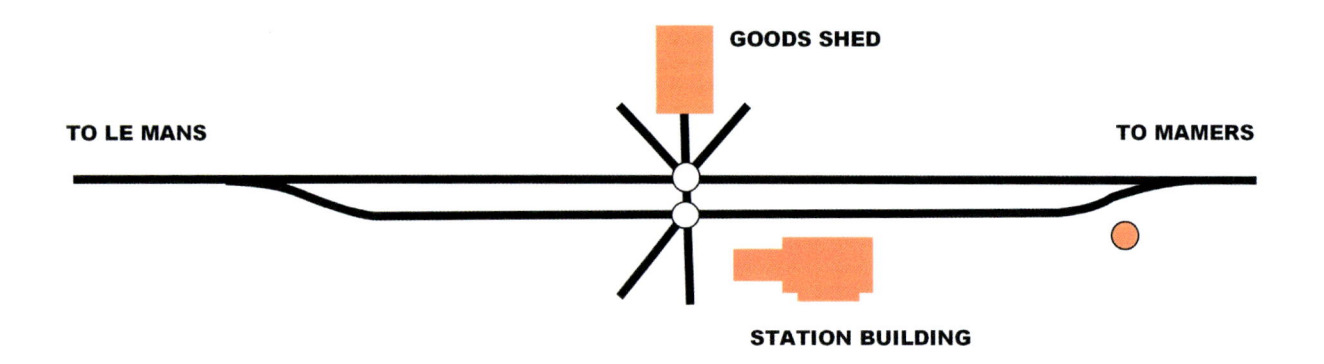

This is the plan of the tramway station, again using turntables which makes it so frustrating for modellers.

The building is superb but looks rather lonely standing in splendid isolation like that. There was a goods shed out of picture on the right.

I can't resist including some pictures of the standard gauge station, it was superb.

BONNETABLE TO MAMERS.

This section was opened in 1888, running north east until it passed the junction station at la Detourbe and then turning north west until reaching the town of Mamers where it terminated by the main line station.

As before the stations have a loop with sidings accessed from turntables. At St Cosme one of the stone buildings has been provided.

At Nogent le Bernard there is quite an array of sidings leading off from the turntables on both sides of the running line, with the loop beginning beyond the turntable in the foreground of the top picture.

The junction station of la Detourbe, with another of the attractive station buildings already seen at Bonnetable. Tracks run to either side of the building and in fact there as a third loop making it a triangular junction to allow through running from any direction.

This café stood adjacent to the station.

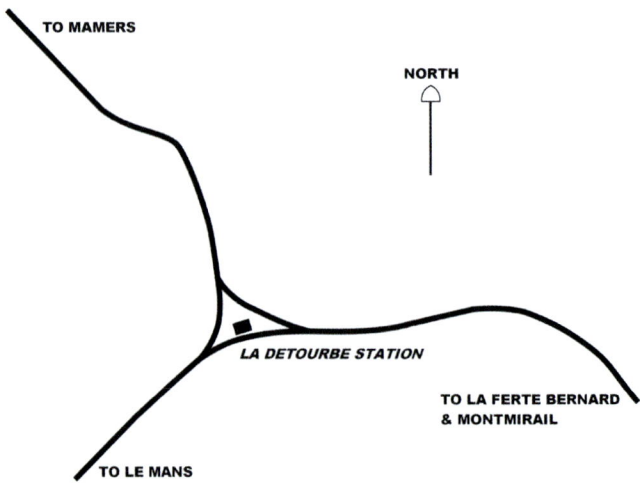

Mamers station, with another of the same design of station building. The tracks in the foreground are the interchange sidings with the standard gauge from St Calais, and the stock is on a standard gauge siding. The wooden goods shed is serving the narrow gauge line, but doesn't appear on the plan of the station so it may have been added later.

MAMERS — Gare du Tramway   F. M.

A OUEST RAILWAY (ETAT)
B SARTHE TRAMWAYS LINE TO ALENCON PARTLY BUILT IN 1916 BUT NEVER FULLY OPENED
C SARTHE TRAMWAYS AND ST CALAIS MAMERS RAILWAY LINE (3 RAIL)

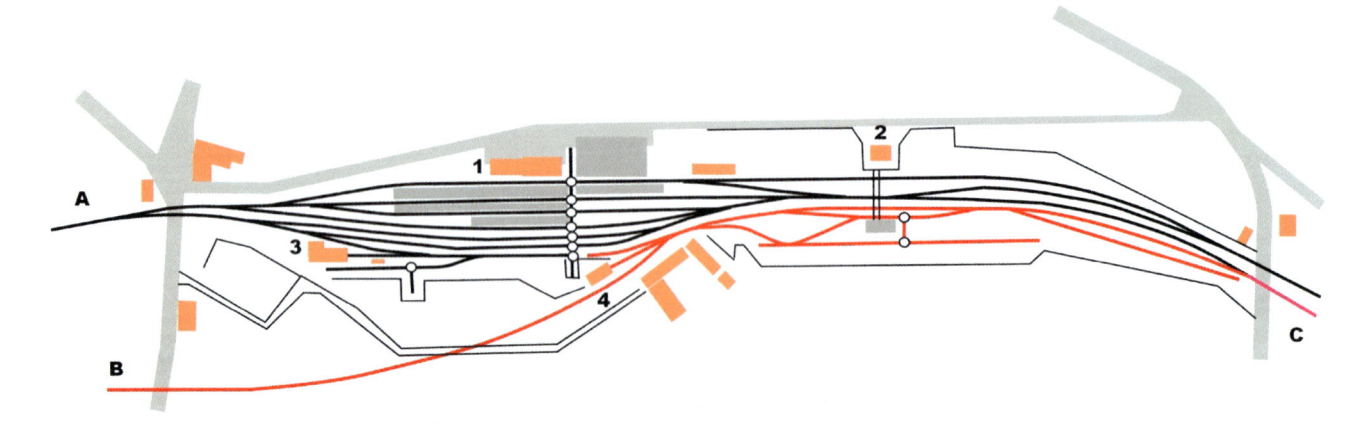

1. OUEST AND ST CALAIS/MAMERS RAILWAY STATION
2. SARTHE TRAMWAYS STATION WITH WALKWAY TO PLATFORM OPPOSITE.
3 STANDARD GAUGE LOCOMOTIVE SHED
4 TRAMWAY LOCOMOTIVE SHED

The St Calais line opened in 1872 and when the tramway was built for the last section into the station the same track was shared by both line as a three rail section.

The line to St Calais closed to passengers in 1965 and to freight in 1977.

The Ouest Railway line between La Hutte and Mortagne shared the station after 1881.

This line was last used in 1994.

LA DETOURBE TO LA FERTE BERNARD.

This section of line ran east from the triangular junction at La Detourbe to the town of la Ferte Bernard, which remained a terminus from opening in 1898 until the line was extended in 1916 to Montmiral. La Ferte Bernard is a town of 9000 people and also has a station on the main line between le Mans and Paris Montparnasse.

This line begins as an perfectly ordinary section of the Sarthe tramways and ends with an exuberant flourish with one of the most amazing narrow gauge stations ever constructed. It was another of de la Noe's creations, of course, but why it should have been built, and in 1888 when money was not plentiful and certainly not to be wasted on decorative excesses, no one seems sure.

I do not have pictures of either of the two intermediate stations, though no doubt they followed the standard pattern for small communities.

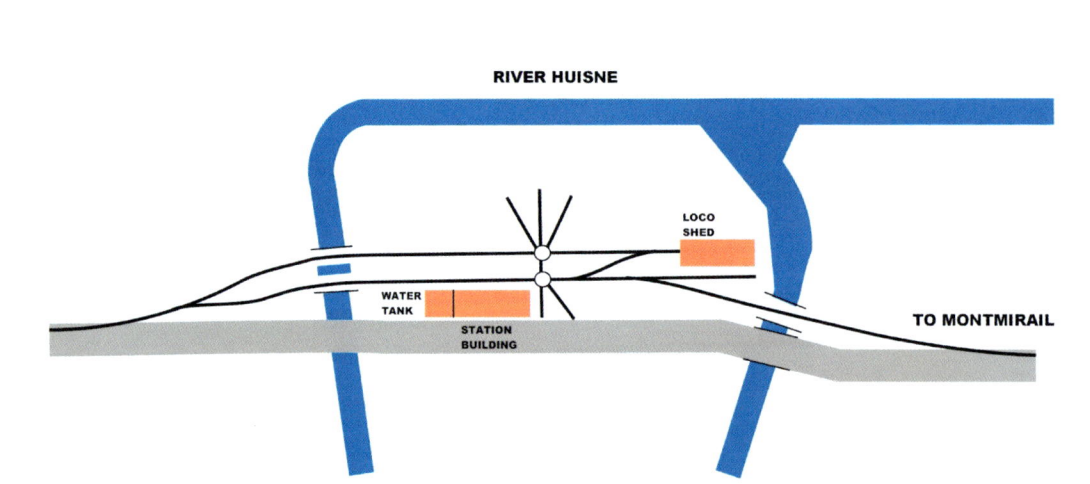

LA FERTE BERNARD STATION

The plan shows the station after the 1916 extension had been built, the line to Montmiral. However, there were no other alterations to the track plan so it's appearance as a terminus remains clear. The line approached from the left running along the side of the road, curving away into the station which lay alongside the river on quite a constricted site.

1897. LA FERTÉ-BERNARD (Sarthe) - Gare des tramways à vapeur

Maybe de la Noe was getting frustrated with all those little shelters, or maybe he just produced this when no one was looking, but what a station! The river bridge is glimpsed in the foreground and beyond is the station building. The nearest part of the structure is the water tank, believe it or not, with the passenger accommodation beyond. On the far side of the road was some of his characteristic brick arched walling, part of which is the only remains still to be seen...the site was cleared in 1949 and a garden was created in it's place.

The picture shows the station as a through station, with the little engine shed on the left.

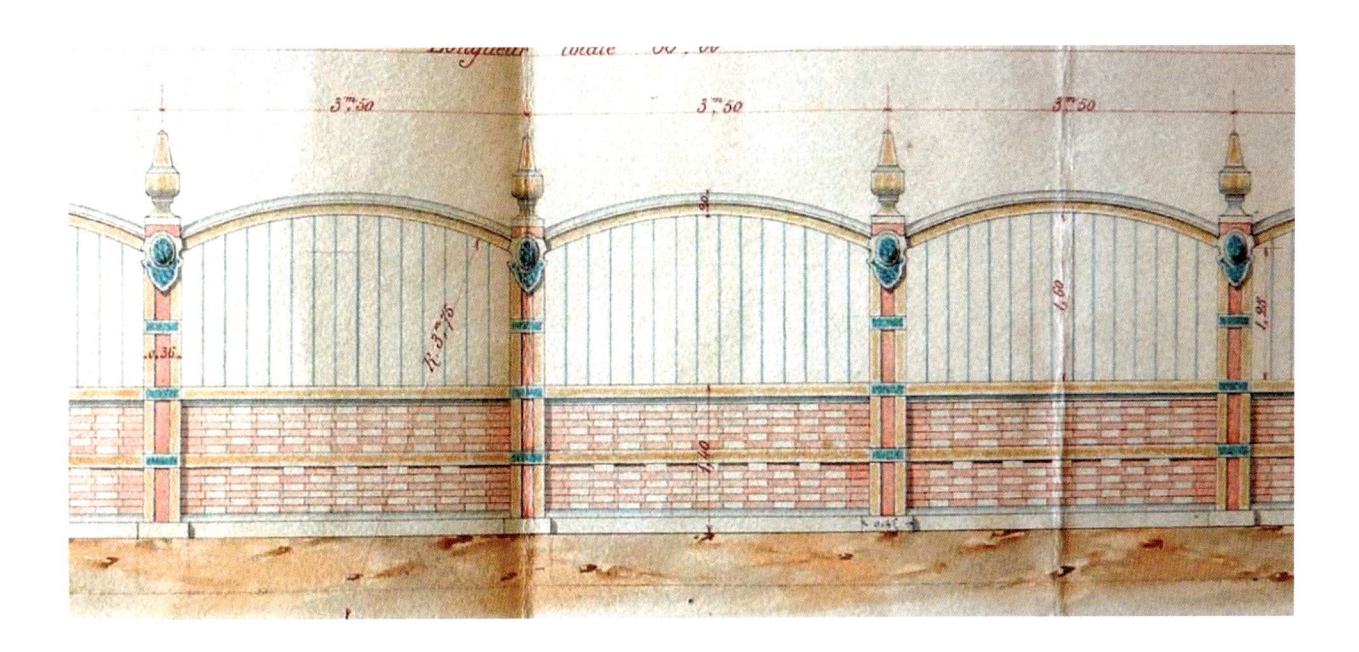

For obvious reasons the station was very widely photographed for postcards.

13. LA FERTÉ-BERNARD (Sarthe)
Gare des Tramways et Avenue de la République

La Ferté-Bernard — Gare du Tramway

Bazar M. Prevost

La Ferté-Bernard. — Gare des Tramways. — Vue d'ensemble

La Ferté-Bernard. — Boulevard de la République et Gare des Tramways

LA FERTÉ-BERNARD (Sarthe) - Gare des Tramways

LA FERTÉ-BERNARD — Gare du Tramway

Edit. Génisson à la Ferté-Bernard, Sarthe

1797. LA FERTÉ-BERNARD (Sarthe) - Gare des tramways à vapeur

The above card shows a siding on the left that does not appear on the track plan; this is a post 1916 picture so it may have been a later addition. It appears to be a loop with another point just outside the engine shed.

Soon after leaving the station, the 1916 extension crossed this low bridge over the river.

La Ferté-Bernard — Le Pont du Boucher

LA FERTE BERNARD TO MONTMIRAIL.

This extension of the line opened in 1915 and has not been well covered photographically—given the date that is hardly surprising.

Theligny station typified those on the line, following the pattern established elsewhere of a loop with short sidings running from a turntable. The station building is one of the attractive brick built structures used across the system.

Saint Ophace station is seen below and was very similar.

The tramway terminated outside the Ouest Railway station at Montmirail, but no pictures have been found of the tramway here. The terminus had the same brick built shelter as the intermediate stations and little more than a run round loop.

Montmirail Ouest station was on the line from Connerre to Orleans which had opened in 1898. It closed to passengers in 1938 and to freight in 1977.

Unfortunately this picture was taken before 1915 but it does show the site of the tramway terminus outside the Ouest station.

LE MANS TO SEGRIE AND BALLON AND FRESNEY TO ALENCON.

The final section of the tramway system to be described was in two separate sections and lay to the north of le Mans; it is coloured black on the map on page 29.

LE MANS TO SEGRIE

The line running north of le Mans to Segrie was one of the later additions to the system, but it connected with one of the first. The short line between Ballons and Montbizot had been open since the 1880's and remained isolated from the main network, though there was an interchange with the standard gauge railway at Montbizot which made the tramway viable.

The line to Segrie opened in 1915 and the Ballon branch was extended to connect with it at St Jean d'Asse. At Segrie there was an interchange with the standard gauge line from Brest to Alencon.

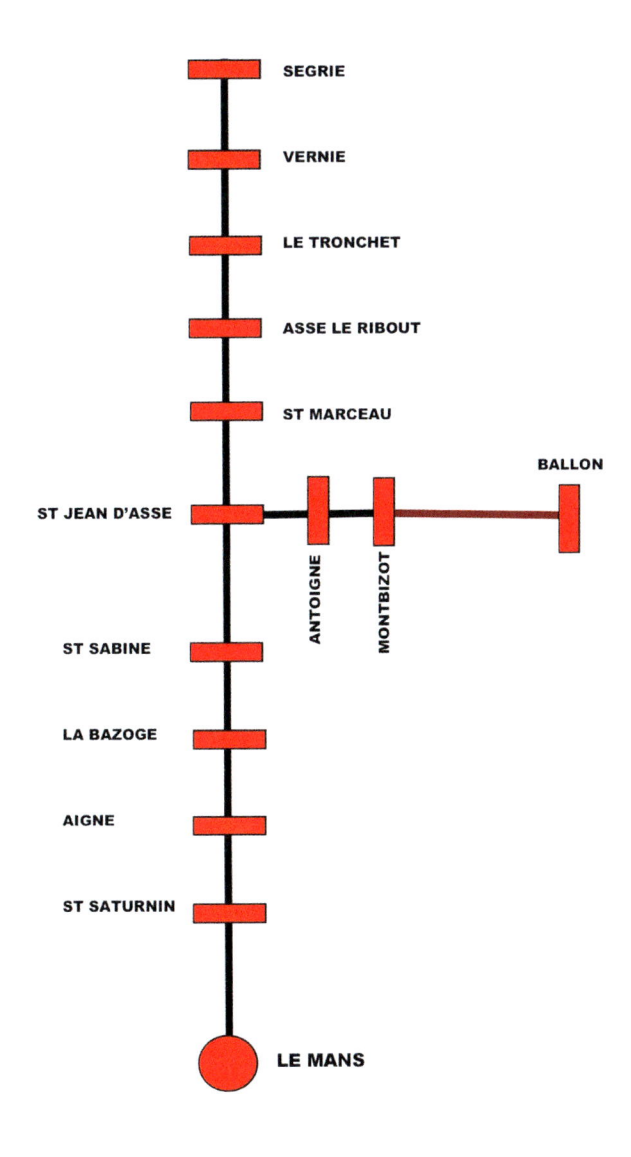

This beautifully restored shelter at St Saturnin is about the only record of any of the stations on the route which passed pretty much unrecorded. I feel better knowing that Claude Wagner couldn't find any pictures either!

This is Segrie Ouest station where the tramway terminated.

It was on the line from Brest to Alencon, opened in 1881. It closed to passengers in 1938 but is still open for freight traffic.

THE BALLON BRANCH

This short line had been built in three parts, the first very short section between Antoigne and the main line station of Montbizot giving an outlet for freight to the main railway which opened in 1882 right at the beginning of the Sarthe tramways. It was extended to the nearby town of Montbizot in 1884 and on to Ballon in 1886; it remained like this, an isolated part of the Sarthe system, until the line to Segrie was opened from le Mans in 1915 with a short branch from it to connect with the Ballon line at Antoigne. Closure came in 1933.

This is the terminus at Ballon, where facilities were not lavish! One of the standard brick shelters was provided, but little else.

The loco is Number 4, a tiny 0-4-T built by Corpet Louvet in 1881 and rarely photographed. They were really too small for the tramways system and no more were ordered after the first batch.

The single coach gives an indication of the amount of traffic to be expected, even on a nice sunny day such as this.

Montbizot (Sarthe). — Gare des Tramways

Montbizot was the most important station on the line which of course until 1915 had to be self contained, hence this large loco shed.

The line ran along the streets of the town in the classic French manner.

4501. MONTBIZOT (Sarthe) — Route de la Gare

Montbizot (Sarthe). — Entrée par route de la Gare

Montbizot (Sarthe). — Avenue de la Gare

The tramway approaching Montbizot Ouest station, seen on the right. This had opened in 1856 and remains in use today.

The delightful picture gives another glimpse of the tramway winding through the streets of Montbizot.

Whether any of this wine came along the tramway to the main station I don't know, but it's too nice a picture not to include.

The line wasn't all bucolic charm, at Antoigne there were sizeable factories including an iron foundry, all feeding traffic onto the tramway.

Montbizot (Sarthe). — Usine d'Antoigné. - Vue Générale

FRESNAY SUR SARTHE TO ALENCON

The final part of the Sarthe Tramways to be described was isolated from the rest of the system, though there were plans to connect it to Segrie which came to nothing.

The line opened in 1914 and ran north from the main line station at Fresnay to terminate outside the Ouest station at Alencon which lies just over the border in the Orne department.

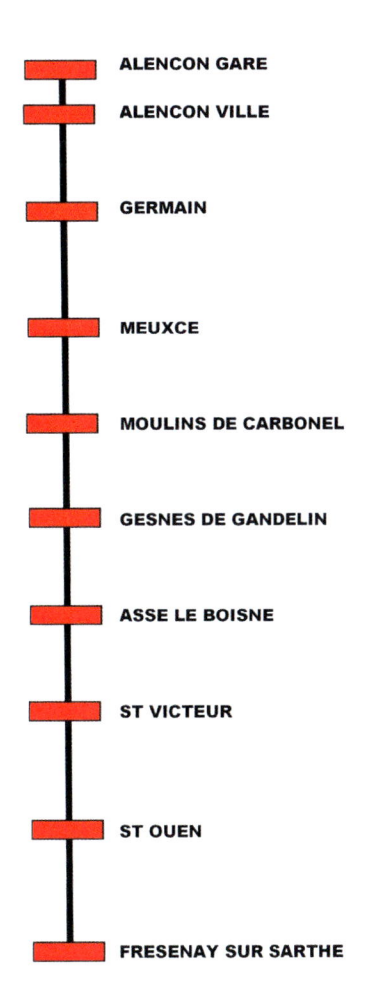

- ALENCON GARE
- ALENCON VILLE
- GERMAIN
- MEUXCE
- MOULINS DE CARBONEL
- GESNES DE GANDELIN
- ASSE LE BOISNE
- ST VICTEUR
- ST OUEN
- FRESENAY SUR SARTHE

Again pictures are very hard to find until Alencon is reached, and that thankfully was reasonably well recorded.

A line connecting Alencon to Mamers was begun in 1916 and construction was well under way before the work was stopped, never to resume.

2805. St-OUEN-de-MIMBRÉ (Sarthe) — Les Carrières, extraction de la pierre

There were large stone quarries at St Ouen, but the internal rail system was 60cm gauge and the stone was taken away on a connection to the standard gauge line close to Fresnay station

Carrière de St-Ouen de Mimbré (Sarthe).

The tramway began outside the Ouest railway station at Fresnay which had opened in 1881. It closed to passengers in 1938.

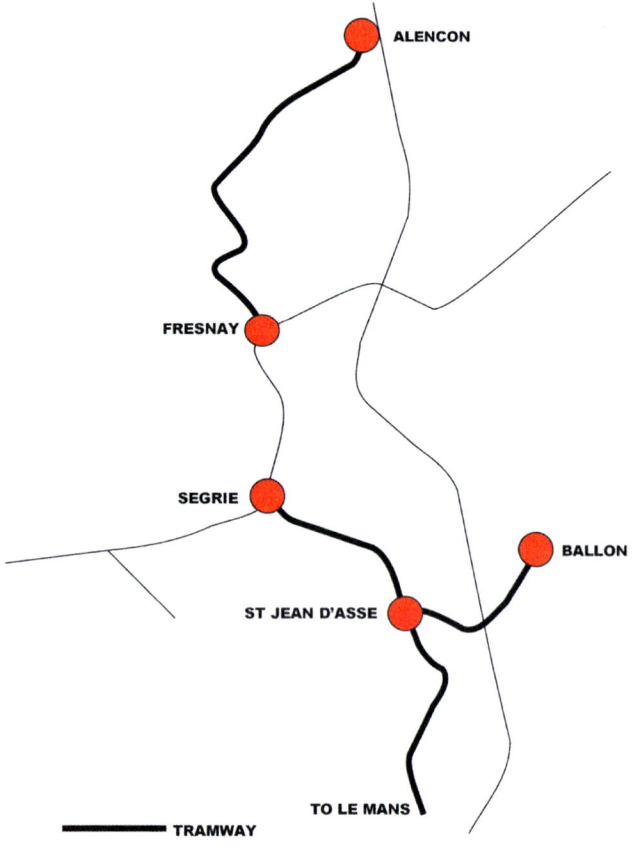

This map shows the lines as built, but had World War One not intervened the two routes would have been joined.

A line was planned to run from Segrie to a new triangular junction station at Asse le Boisne which operationally made perfect sense...the line to Fresnay would then have been a branch off the main route.

Unfortunately the economic situation in the post war period did not allow the project to proceed, the half built line from Alencon to Mamers also being abandoned.

All the planning for the new route had been completed, and drawings exist of the projected triangular junction but it was destined to remain on paper. Had it been built is would not have made a difference to the fortunes of the tramways in terms of delaying their closure.

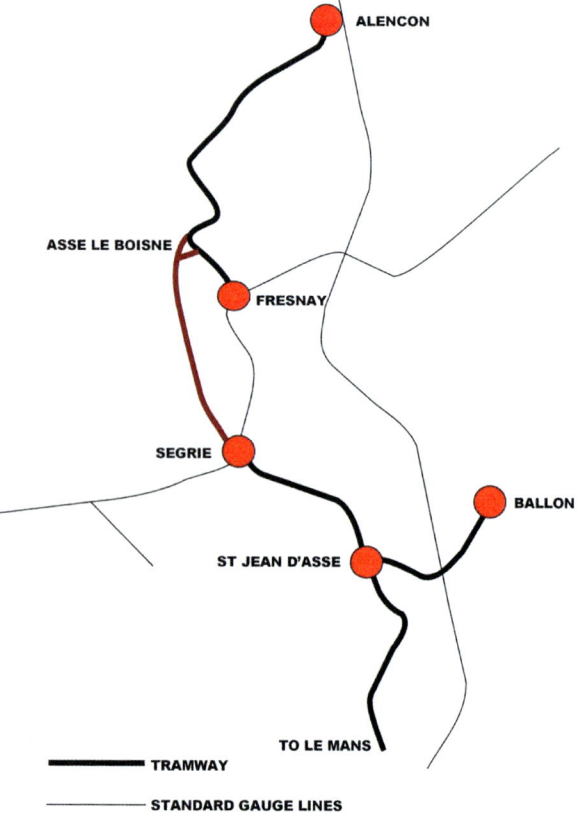

Alencon is an important town and the tramway company spared no expense with their station….a little shelter wouldn't do here. One of the 1912 loco's waits outside having come from the end of the line at the main line station.

The line ran along the road in the time honoured manner. The wooden goods shed stands behind the station building.

116

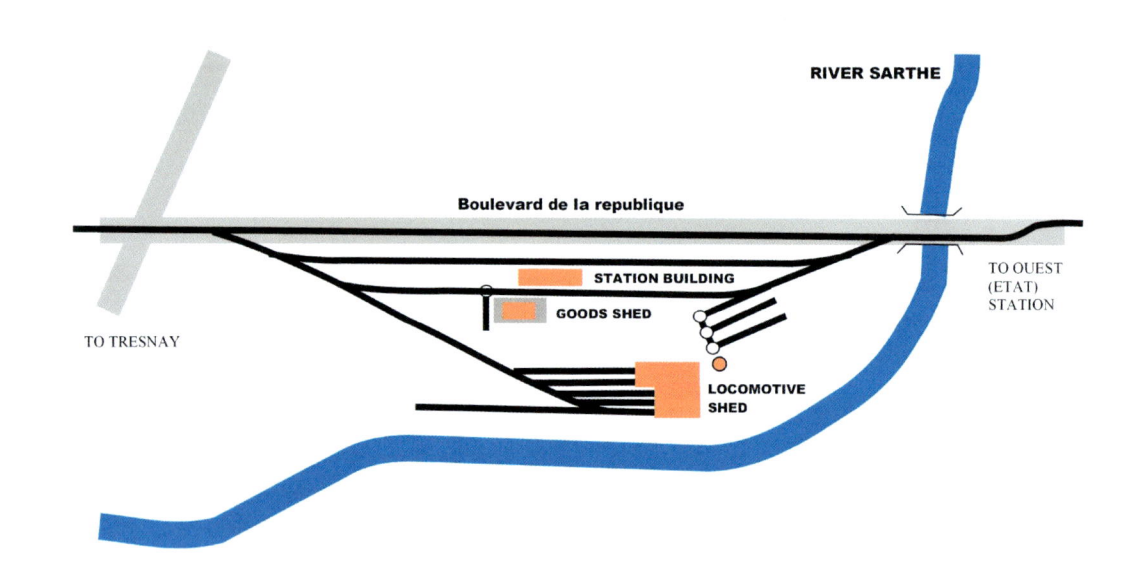

71 ALENÇON. — Intérieur de la Gare. — LL.

Alecenon main line station was opened by the Oeust Railway in 1856, and it became an important junction. It remains open for freight and passengers. The tramway terminated in a passing loop alongside the station forecourt with a single siding from a turntable for freight transfer. The pictures here were taken before the tramway was opened.

92 ALENÇON. — La Gare.

36 — ALENÇON - La Gare
M. C. F. L. Issy (Seine)

The station seen here was destroyed during World War Two and has been replaced by a modern structure.

36. - ALENÇON. - La Gare
Maison des Magasins Réunis, Alençon, éditeur

The Sarthe loco's and stock make lovely models. This is my homage to the tramway in 1/32nd scale.

You may also enjoy these books about French railways:

MAYENNE NARROW GAUGE

THE RAILWAYS OF CHARLEVILLE MEZIERES AND THE FRENCH ARDENNES.

NARROW GAUGE IN THE DROME & VAUCLUSE

THE CHEMINS DE FER DE LA MANCHE.

THE THONES ANNECY TRAMWAY

THE THIZY TRAMWAY

NARROW GAUGE ON THE ILE THE RE.

Printed in Poland
by Amazon Fulfillment
Poland Sp. z o.o., Wrocław